Junior High Game Nights

Wild & Crazy outreach events for junior high ministry

Zondervan/Youth Specialties Books

Adventure Games
Amazing Tension Getters
Attention Grabbers for 4th-6th Graders (Get 'Em Growing)
Called to Care
The Complete Student Missions Handbook
Creative Socials and Special Events
Divorce Recovery for Teenagers
Feeding Your Forgotten Soul (Spiritual Growth for Youth Workers)
Get 'Em Talking
Good Clean Fun
Good Clean Fun, Volume 2
Great Games for 4th-6th Graders (Get 'Em Growing)
Great Ideas for Small Youth Groups
Greatest Skits on Earth
Greatest Skits on Earth, Volume 2
Growing Up in America
High School Ministry
High School TalkSheets
Holiday Ideas for Youth Groups (Revised Edition)
Hot Talks
Ideas for Social Action
Intensive Care: Helping Teenagers in Crisis
Junior High Game Nights
Junior High Ministry
Junior High TalkSheets
The Ministry of Nurture
On-Site: 40 On-Location Programs for Youth Groups
Option Plays
Organizing Your Youth Ministry
Play It! Great Games for Groups
Quick and Easy Activities for 4th-6th Graders (Get 'Em Growing)
Super Sketches for Youth Ministry
Teaching the Bible Creatively
Teaching the Truth about Sex
Tension Getters
Tension Getters II
Unsung Heroes: How to Recruit and Train Volunteer Youth Workers
Up Close and Personal: How to Build Community in Your Youth Group
Youth Ministry Nuts & Bolts
The Youth Specialties Handbook for Great Camps and Retreats
Youth Specialties Clip Art Book
Youth Specialties Clip Art Book, Volume 2

Junior High Game Nights

Wild & Crazy outreach events for junior high ministry

Dan McCollam & Keith Betts

Youth Specialties

Zondervan Publishing House
Grand Rapids, Michigan
A Division of HarperCollinsPublishers

DISCLAIMER

Like life, this book contains games that, in an unfortunate combination of circumstances, could result in emotional or physical harm. Before you use a game, you'll need to evaluate it on its own merits for your group, for its potential risk, for necessary safety precautions and advance preparation, and for possible results. Youth Specialties, Inc., Zondervan Publishing House, and Dan McCollam and Keith Betts are not responsible for, nor have they any control over, the use or misuse of any games published in this book.

Junior High Game Nights

Copyright © 1991 by Youth Specialties, Inc.

Youth Specialties Books, 1224 Greenfield Drive, El Cajon, California 92021,
are published by Zondervan Publishing House,
Grand Rapids, Michigan 49530

Library of Congress Cataloging-in-Publication Data

McCollam, Dan, 1962-
    Junior high game nights: wild and crazy outreach events for junior high
    ministry / Dan McCollam, Keith Betts.
          p.   cm.
    ISBN 0-310-53811-4
    1. Games. 2. Group games. 3. Amusements. 4. Youth—Recreation.
I. Betts, Keith, 1963- . II. Title.
GV1201.M4 1991
793'.0192—dc20
                                                          90-49928
                                                          CIP

Edited by Lundie Carstensen and Kathi George
Designed by Jack Rogers
Typography by Jack Rogers
Illustrated by Corbin Hillam

Printed in the United States of America

96 97 98 99 / ML / 10 9 8 7

To Pastor Cleddie Keith, who believes in doing whatever it takes to win youth into the kingdom of God. Without his support, this book would not exist. May God see fit to raise up others like him.

Special thanks to all the workers and youth sponsors who loved souls enough to make this work and give of themselves. Great is your reward.

CONTENTS

ACKNOWLEDGMENTS

Some of the games in this book were inspired by games that originally appeared in the *Ideas* Library, published by Youth Specialties, Inc.

The authors wish to thank all of the creative youth workers who originally developed these games. Your ideas were a great inspiration to us.

Introduction

Many fantastic game and idea books are available for youth workers today. As youth pastors, you have probably used these resources and have been greatly helped by them. So what makes this collection any different or even necessary?

First of all, we have a different target audience. The games included here are geared to appeal primarily to junior high teens, those between the ages of 11 and 15. Every youth worker knows that the junior higher is an altogether different species. We felt it was necessary to develop a resource that was as outrageous and bizarre as the junior high mind-set. (Quite a challenge!) This game resource is intentionally focused to reach junior high teens.

This idea book also has a different purpose. Other game books have given us great resources for building community, fellowship, and friendship through group play and light competition. The purpose of this book is to give you a resource that will draw in large numbers of unsaved teens. There are only a few actual competitors in each game. The rest of the teens form teams of cheering spectators. This changes the whole nature of the interaction. The games are designed to be fun to watch as well as fun to play. Special attention is given to costume and staging because of the value they add to visual entertainment.

The ideas included here are also quite different in the emphasis given to various aspects of the games. The last few years have seen a huge upsurge in the popularity of teen game shows. We recognized that these game shows all have a few common denominators. One obvious element is the importance of contemporary props, lighting, and sound. Consequently, our first step was to put in stage lighting and a "killer" sound system. We saw a change right away as each game was brightly lit and accompanied by driving Christian music. The teens were pulled right into the games. Another important element to these game shows is crowd response. Therefore, we encouraged the teens to shout, scream, and cheer for the contestants during the games. The teens immediately began to respond like a studio audience, enjoying each game right along with the competitors. Like an audience, they also settled down in quiet anticipation between each competition.

A third element to the games on these shows is more of an emphasis on making a mess than on athletic skill. So we developed wild and messy games: the games are heavy on competition but low on skill. Several games focus on eating contests because they are messy and they are something that everyone is good at. Other competitions are so bizarre that everyone can compete on the same level since no one has any prior experience at the game challenge. We found that such changes in emphasis yield a highly positive response from teens. No longer are we trying to coax teens into participation—they literally line the stage shout-

ing, "Pick me! Pick me!"

Finally, this resource has a bottom line of reaching lost souls. After all, the challenge of youth ministry is not to get teens in or to keep them in, but to see them burst into new life through personal faith in Jesus Christ. For this reason, we have included in this resource an evangelistic message for each night that goes along with the theme. We have found that the games create a real willingness to hear what needs to be said and can therefore serve as an effective evangelistic outreach.

It is our hope now that this resource will be a blessing to you; that you will find it innovative, helpful, and refreshing. Our sincere desire is that, as you use this resource, many souls will be won to the kingdom of God through the foolishness of man.

SECTION ONE

How to Use Junior High Game Nights

Why Games?

This is the question that we asked four years ago when God led us to start an outreach among junior high young people using creative gaming. We were hesitant because it all sounded so social and unspiritual, but God knows best. In the past four years, our little youth group of 30 teenagers has reached out to well over a thousand teens. Over a hundred of these teens are beginning to join themselves to the group through a new relationship with Jesus Christ. Through this experience, God gave us the answer to the question, "Why games?" Here is what we found.

First of all, we found that games meet a genuine need. The Scriptures make it very clear that our Christianity must not just preach doctrine, but should really seek to meet a person's needs. Teens in our culture today are starving for good and wholesome activities in a positive environment. There is so little in the world today that is fun and yet truly wholesome and helpful. If these were starving natives, then I would attempt to feed them; if they were naked, I would clothe them; if they were in prison, I would visit them. I would try to meet their need so that they could meet Jesus. It became obvious to us that our teens were bored and had a legitimate need that had to be met before we would be heard as messengers of the Gospel.

Second, games tear down walls. So often kids come into a youth service bound by troubles and cares. Many of the teens that we work with carry a large responsibility in caring for the needs of their broken families. There is so much on these teens' minds that often it is hard to get through to them, no matter how dynamic the speaker. We have found that good gaming tears down emotional walls by helping teens to laugh, to cheer, to let out a scream, and that somehow then they are really ready to hear. It frees them up to respond to the same truths that we have been sharing all along, but now they are receiving them.

Finally, games open the door to share the Gospel with teens. We have seen kids come to game nights who would never respond to any of our other invitations.

Now that they have come in the door and responded to the message, they are making the choice themselves to attend our teen teaching and worship services. Of course, the game nights could never be the sole program. The wild activities give us the opportunity to get a foot in the door, a chance to meet the teens and their families, and a chance to speak truth into their lives. The games are just a means to an end. The goal is to share Jesus.

Why games? Because teens are ruining their lives out of boredom and silent despair, and games give them something to do that is good, clean fun in a healthy environment. Why games? Because games tear down emotional walls that help kids to hear with a fresh and positive attentiveness. Why games? Because games bring in teens who otherwise might never have heard a gospel that they could relate and respond to. We have been commissioned to go out to the highways and byways and to compel them (give them a reason and a way) to come in. Good creative gaming provides these opportunities.

Small Youth Groups

Just because you have a small youth group, don't set aside *Junior High Game Nights*! You may look at the games in this book and say to yourself, "That is just for big crowds and big churches." Remember that this game program is meant to draw in unsaved teens. Don't look at the number in your youth group; they can be your worker core. Look at the number of kids in your local junior high school: this can be the group you will draw from.

If targeting your junior high school does not seem like it would work, consider challenging another youth group in the area. Combine resources and choose the facility that lends itself best to this kind of program. Challenge several other church groups and ask them to share in the preaching at the end. Remind them that the only message that will ever be preached is the Gospel of the Lord Jesus Christ. Ask several churches in the area to join with you for one semester or a monthly rally. Then plan for the best in outrageous and messy excitement!

If there are no other churches that will or are able to join with you, then check with other youth oriented community groups. Challenge a YMCA group, a boy scout troop, or a big brother program. One year we had two teams from such community groups. One group was a government runaway shelter and the other was a safe place shelter for families in trouble. One social worker who was not a Christian gave us one of the highest recommendations that we received that year!

No matter where you draw your crowd from, ideas from *Junior High Game Nights* will bring a crowd! So don't shut out the opportunity to bring hundreds of bored, troubled, needy, lonely teens into your church or gymnasium for quite possibly the best time they will ever have as a teenager. This program is for you!

Time and Money

"But it sounds involved and expensive!" Good news! The hardest part has already been done for you. All the games you will need are provided for each night. Not only that, the theme is a thread of continuity that keeps things running smoothly and allows you to decorate and plan staging and costumes to add excitement to each night.

Props are an important part of each game night because they really add to the visual excitement. All the props in this book can be made inexpensively out of materials that can be purchased at any local toy, novelty, or hardware store. We spent about $30 per game night for props and all this expense was recovered through an offering.

If you are stranded in the boondocks where these supplies are just not available, then fear not. All of the items in this book can be ordered through toy and novelty catalogues. Here are two that we have used:

Acme Premium Supply: 800-325-7888
Kipp Brothers Inc.: 800-428-1153

Since all the props are listed in the book, you can order them in advance. The discount you will get by ordering factory direct can also more than make up for any shipping costs. Our experience has been that these companies provide fast, efficient service with no back orders.

As far as being involved, yes, it takes some work to pull off a great game night. But this book gives you a head start. You choose the night that is best for you. Monday night was an extremely effective night for us because there were few schedule conflicts and teens are generally bored on Monday nights. We found that by holding our game nights on Mondays, school attendance actually went up on Mondays in the public school! Instead of being the dreaded "Blue Monday" for

many teens, it was actually the highlight of their week. The bottom line is that it is your decision. We have created twelve game nights that will work weekly, monthly, or even just occasionally. This book was created to serve you. You can make the program work to fit your situation.

Food Games and Starving Children

We have great compassion toward the world hunger effort. We also realize that there are teens on every block in America who are starving. Their bellies may be full but their hearts are very empty. In this "couch potato" generation, fewer kids are athletic than ever before. Because of the collapse of the nuclear family, teenagers also face an epidemic of inferiority. For some kids, the only contest that they could ever win is an eating contest. You should see the smile that comes across a chubby little teen's face as he wins a contest for his team. Christianity meets the total need of humanity. Feed all the hungry and don't write off the food games. They may be the only contests that some little boy will ever win.

As far as hunger outreach goes, every year our game program sponsors a "Get Your Can to (program name) Night." To get in the building that night, the teens must all bring canned goods. We award points to the team that brings in the most cans. Included in the games are can-stacking contests and mystery-can eating games where the labels are peeled off and the contestant must eat whatever is inside. Last year in this effort, we were able to supply each of 80 families with three grocery bags stuffed with food at Thanksgiving time. For most of these families, it was the only way they could have celebrated a traditional Thanksgiving holiday.

On the Safe Side

Some games you will want to test out before you try them in a live situation with kids. This can be done in advance with volunteers. Testing out a game before you use it helps all workers and stage hands to visualize what will take place. When a game variation is suggested, this will help you decide which variation would be best for you. We have also found that the workers enjoy experiencing the games, and so it is both fun and educational.

Tips on Trashing Your Church

"How do you get away with making such a mess of the church?" We have a great head pastor who has allowed us to do whatever it takes to win other teens to Jesus. But there are some precautions that you can take.

1. Cover your stage or play area with tarps or drop cloths and tape or fasten them down each week. Check with hardware stores or tent and awning companies for a good, heavy polyvinyl tarp that will last you through the year. This protection is well worth the initial investment and will protect your floor or carpet from any damage.

2. Choose a location that has bathrooms or changing rooms directly off the stage area. When teens finish a messy competition, don't allow them to walk out into the audience; escort them directly to these cleanup areas.

3. Assign two or three teens to be stagehands for the entire semester. Their job is to hustle tables, chairs, and other props on and off stage and to clean up after each contest. If there is a cleanup crew clearing the stage while you announce the next stunt, then the overall mess is kept under better control.

4. The slogan for our game nights was "Dress for the mess!" This prepared teens for the nature of the games and protected us from any accusations of damage to their clothes. We found this also served the purpose of breaking down fashion cliques, since no one was wearing labels—everyone was just in old jeans and T-shirts.

If your church does not have a facility suitable for such a program, then check into renting or borrowing a hall or gymnasium on a regular basis. One summer, we ran the program outside in a tent on the church grounds. This also was a great success. Don't give up if you can't have it in your church; there is a place in your community where you can make it work.

Bringing Them In

All youth workers have their own methods of promotion, visitation, and follow-up. Let us merely share with you here a method that was successful for us. Since we held our game nights on Mondays, we would have all our workers and volunteers gather on Saturday mornings. At this meeting we would pray and work out any problems with them. This was also a time of reinforcing the vision of the games program, which for us was "mass evangelism and one-on-one discipleship." After an hour meeting, we would send each volunteer out with brightly colored flyers (with cartoons from clip art books) announcing the theme and special events or prizes. The workers would visit each teen who had come in the last week and give each of them the next week's flyer. They would also visit ten new teens each week through contacts made during the week or names given by the regular attendees. This door-to-door, personal visitation will help promote attendance, advance follow-up, and increase your number of weekly visitors.

Costumes, Embarrassment, and Coming Back

"You talk a lot about costumes . . . what's the deal?" Believe it or not, we found that teens still love to dress up. Every week became a costume contest where we would award extra points to those that dressed for the theme. Dressing for the theme also helped the kids to get into the program before they ever got there. They were so excited about their costumes that we could have done just about anything and they would have loved it because their hearts were already into it.

Costume and prop suggestions are provided for each theme. The value of costumes is amazing. We have all seen the old pie-eating contest done with no hands. It's funny, but it isn't anything new. Several of the games in this book are just a twist on an old theme: you put a bunch of plastic pig noses on your contestants and suddenly the pie contest becomes a pigging out contest and everyone looks silly before they ever get started. It adds to the fun, it adds to the humor, and it gives kids a mask to hide behind that can actually make them feel more comfortable.

"Yeah . . . but don't you embarrass teens?" Junior high teens are already embarrassed. They are the victims of pu-berty and it is playing some pretty dirty tricks on them. Games like these and the crazy costumes help teens to laugh at themselves. With all the hype, the cheering, the clapping, and the shouting, we encourage each teen contestant. In this way, teens are both laughing at themselves and affirming one another. That is why we encourage you to hold a rowdy, flashy, prop-filled night of fun!

"Do teens come back when the games are over?" Game nights are definitely not a cure-all. As a matter of fact, these programs are just seeds. Scripture tells us that the Gospel is a seed. What happens to that seed after it has been sown depends on many variables. What we have tried to do is make the game nights one of the best memories that a teen will ever have. Later, when that teen is hurting and in trouble, we believe that he or she will remember that the happiest time was in church. Teens will remember the people who went out of their way to show them a good, fun time. Our goal is to provide you with a seed that can bring a great harvest in your community.

To Preach or Not to Preach?

Don't be afraid to preach and don't settle for just drawing a crowd! Give teens something that they can take home. Preach the Gospel. If you get off on issues, then your game night has ceased to be an evangelistic outreach. For each game night we have provided an evangelistic message. We believe the games are tempting enough to bring back a crowd and we believe that the Gospel is the power of God unto salvation! Preach the Word with boldness, clarity, and simplicity, and expect great results.

Working It into Your Calendar

Junior High Game Nights can be used effectively on a weekly, monthly, or quarterly basis. There are benefits to each calendar choice. Obviously, quarterly game nights allow you the most time to prepare, promote, follow up, and sometimes recover. This may be the best choice for a volunteer or part-time youth worker. The quarterly calendar choice also allows you the time to do these events on a larger scale. You may want to bring in a guest speaker or artist; or you may want to combine this with an existing quarterly rally or sectional rally. In selecting the quarterly choice, you have in this volume three years of the wildest tried-and-true gaming ideas for reaching junior high teens, and the time and resources to execute them with excellence!

Junior High Game Nights also work great as part of a monthly program. Teens like the security of a routine and it gives them something to look forward to. The monthly choice allows you the time to advertise in monthly newsletters and magazines and to use your prefab "Coming This Month" clip art. Perhaps the greatest advantage of the monthly choice is that it gives you a regular fun event that boosts your attendance and reaches out to the lost without interrupting your regular weekly activities. This choice means you have one full year of great gaming ideas in this volume.

The weekly choice is for kamikaze youth workers, like us, who like to have a million things going at once. "Never give them time to say, 'I'm bored,'" is our motto. You will find that *Junior High Game Nights* is complete enough to supply all you need to pull off these games on a weekly basis with only minimal brain damage. For those of you who choose this calendar option, we have several suggestions:

1. Get plenty of help from youth sponsors, volunteers, and your key teens.

2. You may want to use a cohost to help keep things running smoothly on stage. This cohost can also share in many of the preparation responsibilities.

3. Remember to balance your program with other activities, such as opportunities for follow-up, Bible study, one-on-one, and worship.

4. Divide your game nights into six- to nine-week semesters with breaks in between to regroup, revive, recover, and refocus.

5. Buy the family-size aspirin bottle at your local supermarket.

The weekly calendar choice offers dynamic growth, high momentum, and an explosive impact on the community that advertises itself. You may want to run your semesters concurrent with the school year, leaving ample time off for spring break and holiday seasons. Although with this choice you have only one or two semesters of material, have no fear, because *More Junior High Game Nights* will be coming your way in spring 1992!

SECTION TWO

Junior High
Game Nights

1. The Bizarre B-Ball Bash

COSTUMES, PROPS, AND PROMOTION

Costumes: Encourage teens to wear team T-shirts or basketball uniforms. Anything that has to do with basketball could win bonus "team spirit" points. Teens could bring basketballs, posters, player cards, or even wear a backboard and hoop. The wilder the idea and the greater the participation, the more generous you should be in giving team spirit or rally points. You also may make it your policy to choose only contestants for competitions who come in costume.

Props: Lay out all props on the stage to heighten interest and curiosity as the teens enter. You may want to decorate the room with basketball posters, streamers, balloons, or school basketball trophies. Otherwise, the game props should provide adequate decoration.

Promotions: Advertise the world's biggest basketball game. You can take this promotion as far as your imagination allows. Contact the area newspapers or local television networks. This is also a great chance to invite a Christian basketball star to be your guest speaker. Don't forget to consider local heroes or college athletes who have taken a stand for Christ. Invite a junior high championship team to be your special guest; or you could invite a local coach, a college scout, or a cheerleading squad to visit. You might want to check with your local chapter of Fellowship of Christian Athletes or Athletes in Action for a special guest speaker. The possibilities are endless. You decide—take it as far as you want to go and let the program work for you.

A GAME OF P*I*G

Materials:

Prepare paper wads for each player to shoot baskets with. About 20 paper wads per player is ideal. The target or basket will be an ordinary wastebasket. Prepare a nonmenthol shaving cream pie in advance and keep it hidden.

The Challenge:

Announce that you are going to start off the night by playing an ordinary game of P*I*G using paper wads and a wastebasket. Ask for one volunteer from each team, preferably boys or girls who are fairly good shots. Make sure that they are also good sports. It's best not to use a first-time visitor for this game. If you are using several teams or contestants, then have a free throw contest—the best out of ten shots—to narrow the competition down to just two players. When you have your two shooters, pick one to go first and set the shot. That same shot must be made by the second shooter or he or she is assigned the letter "P." If the first player misses the shot, then the second player is allowed to set the shot. Each time a shot is made, the same shot must be made by the competitor or a letter is awarded.

When a player receives a letter, bring both contestants to the front of the stage. Place your hand on the neck of the leading player and bring him or her to the front of the stage. Ask the audience, "Now what does this player have?" They will yell back, "Nothing!" Place your hand on the neck of the other player and bring him or her forward to ask the crowd, "And what does this player have?" They yell back, "He has a P!" Remind the players that the first one to get the letters "P*I*G" is out and the other player wins. Remember to ask the audience these questions each time a player gets a letter.

Now, when a player gets a "P*I," he or she is still expecting to get another turn. Again, go through the motions of bringing the shooters forward to ask the crowd what they have. Start with the winning player: "Now what does this player have?" The crowd will give the appropriate response. Place your hand on the neck of the player with the "P*I" and bring him or her forward. While you keep this player looking at the crowd, have someone sneak up behind with the shaving cream pie.

Ask the audience, "Now what does this

player have?" They yell back, "He has P*I!" By now the crowd is figuring out what is taking place. Now ask them, "And what does that spell?" The crowd yells back, "Pie!" Just then the pie is thrown gently into the shooter's face. Name the other shooter the winner and give bonus points to the losing shooter for being a finalist and for being a good sport!

DOUBLE DRIBBLE

Materials:

You will need two 16-ounce bottles of Coke for each contestant. Tape the bottles together in the middle, winding duct tape around them several times.

The Challenge:

Bottle caps are removed. At a signal, players must tip the bottle and attempt to drink both bottles of Coke at the same time. Players may not plug one bottle. The player to drink both Cokes the fastest without double dribbling them all on the floor is the winner.

"EGGSPERIENCED" PLAYERS ONLY

Materials:

You have two tried-and-true options here.

Option 1: Buy some army helmets at your local toy store and attach small Nerf hoops to the front of them with small bolts or Super Glue. In this game, one player wears the hoop helmet while the other player shoots baskets with eggs. The one with the most goals wins.

Option 2: Assemble four rectangular banquet tables standing on end so that the tabletop is perpendicular to the floor. At the top of these tables, attach a standard-size Nerf hoop using the suction cup ends. Use colored electrical or masking tape to mark off a backboard square.

The Challenge:

Choose one contestant for each basketball goal you have prepared. Allow them to practice shooting baskets using Nerf balls. Have a dozen eggs for each shooter and keep them hidden. Ask which girls in the audience really believe that their team's contestant is the most "egg-sperienced" player. When several girls raise their hands, choose one to sit underneath the goal to count the number of baskets scored. When you have all the girls positioned underneath the baskets with their backs resting against the table-top, bring out the eggs! Remind the girls that they had great confidence in their player and that if he swishes the hoop with the egg, then no yolk should get on them. Of course if he misses, the egg will hit the table and the raw egg will slide down onto the girls' heads. As the girls sit beneath the baskets, the boys have a shoot-off until all the eggs are gone. Girls and a spotter count baskets to award a winner, but the "yoke" is definitely on the girls!

TEAM BASKETBALL BASH

Materials:

Attach a sharp pin, a hat pin, or a clean nail to the end of a single volleyball pole or free-standing sports pole. Fill a punch balloon (a large balloon attached to a rubber band) three-fourths of the way full with air. Place the lip of the balloon over a can of foam shaving cream and continue to inflate until full. Tie off the balloon.

The Challenge:

Several players from each team surround the popping pole. The punch balloon is thrown into play by an official. The balloon is then batted around with each player trying to score a basket by knocking the balloon onto the pin at the top of the pole. Play continues until the balloon pops. Upon contact with the pin, shaving cream sprays all the contestants. Prepare extra balloons and play several rounds. This is sure to be a favorite.

THE THRILL OF VICTORY AND THE AGONY OF DE'FEET

Materials:

You will need one or more judges with a good nose and a strong stomach.

The Challenge:

You guessed it. Yes, this is a smelly feet contest. Have judges move through each team to pick one "rank" volunteer from every team. Representatives then come to the front of the stage and are seated for the final judging. Award points and a box of Odor Eaters to the winner.

Another variation is to have contestants pass their basketball sneakers forward for judging. Although this may be less embarrassing for the teen, it is much worse for the judges.

THE WORLD'S BIGGEST BASKETBALL GAME

Materials:

Attach a large hula hoop to a 4' x 8' sheet of plywood that has been painted white. This will be your backboard and rim. Support the hula hoop with kite string that can be thumbtacked to the plywood to hold the hula hoop rim at a 90-

degree angle to the plywood backboard. Hang fishnet from the hula hoop rim to form a hoop net. You now have a completed basketball goal for the world's biggest basketball game. Make another goal using the same process. Hang one of these goals in a high corner at either end of the building. Purchase a four-foot beach ball as your giant basketball. These are available at most local toy stores. Some stores carry giant four-foot inflatable globes, which add to the pun of the "World's Biggest Basketball Game."

The Challenge:

Clear away all the tables, chairs, or other obstacles in the room. Divide the group into two teams. The beach ball may be bounced, dribbled, rolled, or passed. The only illegal motion is to run with the ball: that is a traveling violation and the other team will get to take over possession of the ball. This game is best when there are no boundaries. Play the ball off the walls, off the ceiling, and off the stage. Each basket is worth one point. There are no fouls and no free throws.

You are the referee and possession of the ball may be surrendered to the other team at any time for unnecessary roughness. The winner is the first team to have five points. It is best to save this event as the final competition of the night.

A variation is to leave players seated facing the stage and hang a single basketball goal at the front of the stage. All teams compete at the same time, trying to score the first basket. Players must stay fully seated in their chairs. To rise out of the chair constitutes a "bun violation." The whistle is blown by a referee and possession of the ball is surrendered to another team. Play continues until the first basket is scored. You may want to use more than one ball and you probably should use more than one referee.

TONIGHT'S MESSAGE: TRUSTING THE ONE WITH EXPERIENCE

Scripture: Luke 6:46-49.

Introduction:

Tonight we had girls come forward who trusted the experience and the ability of the one shooting. They were surprised to find out that it was going to cost them more than just saying, "I believe." Christianity is like that. There are many of us that would say, "I believe in God," but when it really comes down to trusting him with the decisions of our lives, the cost is too great. We put conditional trust in God.

Illustration:

"Lord, I will go anywhere but Africa"; "Lord, I'll do anything but tell my friends at school about you"; "Lord, you can

have everything but this one thing (a girlfriend, boyfriend, job, car)." That kind of conditional trust is actually *unbelief*. With their mouths they say they believe, they call him Lord, but they won't back it up with their lifestyles.

Focus:

Jesus presents this question to a group of people who were living a lie of unbelief, "Why do you call me, 'Lord, Lord,' and do not do what I say?" In other words, "Why do you say you believe in me, but you don't really trust me or follow me?" He then gives us a parable that teaches us *three things about this kind of person.*

1. The house looks the same. Both

men in the story built a house. To all appearances it probably seemed that the houses were the same, but on the inside one house had no foundation. A lot of people are like that in the church. On the outside they may look exactly the same. They may profess to be Christians, but on the inside they know that their house—their life—is not really built upon Christ. Don't be deceived just because the houses look the same.

2. The storms were the same. The Bible does not promise that there will be no storms for the Christian. As a matter of fact, this parable suggests that the same storms will hit all of us in life. The storm that hit the house with the solid foundation was no different than the storm that hit the other house. Only the end result was different.

3. Ultimately the house without foundation will fall. The fall of one who has built his life without a real foundation in Christ is inevitable. It is sure to come and the collapse will be complete. There is no promise for a house half standing. We must be completely surrendered to Christ.

Conclusion:

Is your life really built on the foundation of Christ? Are you ready to back up your belief with your life, no matter what the cost? On the outside you may look the same as everyone else. Only you know what foundation your life is really built on. Will the faith you profess stand the test of the storms of life? Are you ready to be completely surrendered to Christ and his will? Decide tonight!

2. Medical Madness

COSTUMES, PROPS, AND PROMOTION

Costumes: Invite the teens to wear hospital attire of any kind. They can come as nurses, doctors, surgeons, or patients. You may want to award bonus points for the person who comes with the worst fake injury; junior high teens will really get creative with that. If participation is slow or slack, try offering a cash prize for the best costume or injury. Remember that you can also choose to allow only those who come in costume to compete in the games.

Props: Position all game props and materials on the stage to heighten interest as teens come in. You may want to decorate the area behind the stage with white sheets that have a red cross painted on them. You can also decorate the back wall with old crutches, casts, wheelchairs, or other hospital gear.

Promotions: Advertise the "Patient Races." Note that other groups may have had wheelchair races, but you are going to take it a step further. Invite teens to come prepared to race on crutches, in wheelchairs, or in casts. You will find that some teens will even be practicing and training for this event. You may want to invite a Christian doctor or nurse to be your guest speaker. Make sure that they understand your program and that their portion of the program should be brief and challenging. Another possibility is to invite a paramedic or rescue squad worker who is a born-again Christian. These specialists can often have an impact on teens about both the frailty and the fragility of life.

HOP AND POP

Materials:

Purchase a dozen white surgical gloves from your local pharmacy for about 5¢ apiece. Inflate the surgical gloves like balloons, half full of air and half full of water or shaving cream. Tie off the surgical gloves as you would a normal balloon. Suspend surgical glove balloons from a rope about six feet off the ground using kite string to connect the gloves to the rope. Attach a large hat pin or skewer to the top of a toy doctor's surgical reflector or a nurse's cap. These will be used to pop the balloons.

The Challenge:

At a signal, the doctors or nurses put on the popping devices and attempt to hop and pop four of the surgical glove balloons in front of their team. Each time a balloon is popped, the shaving cream or water showers the contestant. The winner is the first teen to pop all four surgical glove balloons.

I.V. DRINK

Materials:

Purchase some clear tubing from your local hardware store. You will need about four feet of tubing for each contestant. This tubing is very inexpensive and can also be purchased from a pet store that sells fish tank aerators. Stick one end of the tubing into the top of a one-gallon Ziploc storage bag. Fill the bag with one liter of Cherry 7-Up and zip it shut. These are your I.V. bags; they can be hung from a pole, or hanger, or held by a nurse during the competition.

The Challenge:

Suspend the I.V. bags slightly above the patient. Have the patients put the other end of the small clear tubing in their mouths. At a signal, players begin slurping down the 7-Up. The first patient to drain an I.V. bag is the winner.

MOM'S MEDICINE

Materials:

Our local pharmacy donated four giant empty prescription bottles. These bottles may also be purchased. The bigger the bottles, the better. Fill the prescription bottles with strawberry shakes from a local fast food restaurant. Also, provide each team with a huge serving spoon.

The Challenge:

Everyone remembers a time when, as a child, they were forced to take medicine that they really didn't want. The pill always seemed too big to swallow or the spoon larger than could ever fit in your mouth. In remembrance of those times, choose one player to a be a mother and one to be the patient from each team. At a signal, the mothers pour a spoonful of medicine into the patient. Make sure the spoons are big enough so that the players cannot fit them in their mouths. Patients are not allowed to drink from the bottle. Mothers keep spooning out the medicine until the bottle is empty. The first one to finish off the bottle wins.

MUMMY WRAP

Materials:

Supply each team with two rolls of multi-ply toilet paper. The heavy generic brands work great.

The Challenge:

Choose two players from each team to be nurses. At a signal, the nurses mummify a patient as quickly as possible, using the entire roll of toilet paper as a bandage.

A great game variation is to give each team four nurses and four rolls of toilet paper. At a signal, nurses begin to mummify or "TP" the whole team where it is seated. The winner in each contest is the first team of nurses to use all of the mummy wrap.

PATIENT RACES

Materials:

Provide a roll of wrap-type bandages or wide athletic tape for each contestant. You can also provide crutches and wheelchairs or invite teens to bring them from home.

The Challenge:

Wrap bandages or athletic tape firmly around the legs of each team's player, binding both legs from the ankles to the knees. At a signal, players hop, jump, or shuffle toward the finish line as fast as they can. At the finish line, they can tag off with a runner on crutches who will then race back to the starting point. Once there, they can tag off with a patient in a wheelchair, who then races back to the finish line. The first team to complete the race is the winner.

You also can have all the patients race at one time to see who is faster: the cast, the crutches, or the wheelchair. Bandages can be held tight with athletic or masking tape.

SPONGE BATH

Materials:

Provide several large sponges and two buckets for each team. Fill one bucket up with water.

The Challenge:

Choose six players from each team. Position two of each set of players in front of their own teams with the buckets and the sponges. The remaining four players from each team will each be positioned at the four corners of their team's seating area. At a signal, the first player dunks a sponge in the bucket of water and tosses it clockwise to the first corner person. Each corner person tosses the sponge around the perimeter of the team until it is tossed back up to the last person who wrings out the remaining water in the empty bucket. The dry sponge is then handed back to the starting player to be dunked and put back in play. The more sponges you have in play at one time, the greater the excitement. Remember to have loud contemporary music going during the competition. At the end of one song, the winning team is the one to have wrung the most water into the empty bucket. Meanwhile, the whole audience has received a light sponge bath. This is a great team game and everyone is likely to have fun getting wet.

TONIGHT'S MESSAGE: THE SECOND TOUCH

Scripture: Mark 8:22-26.

Introduction:

There are many great stories of healing in the Bible, but one of my favorites is the story Mark tells of the blind man who needed a second touch. The first touch brought vision, but he needed a second touch from Jesus to add clarity and focus.

In some ways I think Job had a second touch in his life. His first confession was, "I spoke of things I did not understand, things too wonderful for me. . . . My ears had heard of you but now my eyes have seen you" (Job 42:3, 5). Job's first touch was when he believed in God because of what he had heard. He received a second touch when he had a personal encounter with God himself.

Focus: *We all need a second touch.*

1. In our lives. It is easy to lose sight of what is really important in this life.

There are so many things that surround us every day that it is easy to look at that which is temporal rather than that which is eternal. It is easy to worry about what we shall eat and wear and do rather than seeking first his kingdom and righteousness (Matthew 6:25-33). We need a second touch to focus our eyes again on what is really important in life.

2. In our dealings with others. It is amazing how quickly we can turn our attention back toward self. Christ said, "If anyone would come after me, he must **deny himself** and take up his cross and follow me" (Matthew 16:24). In a world that is completely preoccupied with self and pleasure, we definitely need a second touch to focus our attention on reaching out to and truly loving others.

3. In our relationships with God. Perhaps you are like Job. You have believed in God because you have heard so many good things about him. The Bible commends you when it says, ". . . blessed are those who have not seen and yet have believed" (John 20:29). Still, it may be that you have never really established a personal relationship of love and trust with the Lord. It is time for your second touch.

Conclusion:

Has your eyesight been dimmed since God first touched you? Have you lost focus about what is truly important in life? Or, have you never really had the personal encounter with God that sealed your relationship with him? Come tonight for a second touch!

3. The Great Escape

COSTUMES, PROPS, AND PROMOTION

Costumes: Encourage the teens to come in convict attire, striped shirts and pants, or guard and police uniforms.

Props: Stack all your props on center stage to heighten interest as teens come in. You may want to decorate the back wall behind your stage with black streamers, hanging them vertically to look like bars of a jail cell. You will also find that

there are many contemporary Christian songs that deal with breaking out and escaping sin. These should be chosen and cued in advance for use during the competitions.

Promotions: There are several great slogan ideas you can use for promoting this event. We used a poster with a teenager chained to his homework. The copy read,

"The Great Escape—Break Into Fun!" There are many variations you can create using the breaking out theme. This game night also works very well in conjunction with seasonal changes, such as "Break into Summer with the Great Escape!"

BALL AND CHAIN GAME

Materials:

Supply each player with a fully inflated black balloon. Using a 24-inch piece of kite string, tie one end to the balloon and the other to the player's ankle.

The Challenge:

Once signaled to start, players try to stomp on other players' balloons while they keep their own from being popped. The last player with his or her balloon still inflated is the winner. A variation of the game is to have players try to pop their own balloons and thus free themselves from the ball and chain.

CAKE 'N' FILE

Materials:

Prepare normal cake batter for four small cakes. Place a file in the batter. You can use an emery board as your file. With the file in the bottom of each cake, bake them at regular temperature. Let the cakes cool, then frost them. Provide cheap plastic handcuffs for each team.

The Challenge:

Seat contestants at a table. Handcuff the players' hands behind their backs. At a signal, the players begin to eat the cake, searching for the file. Obviously players cannot use their hands. The first player to come up with a file in his or her teeth is the winner.

HANDCUFF ESCAPE

Materials:

You will need one set of metal handcuffs for each contestant.

The Challenge:

Have players kneel down with their hands behind their backs. Tape the players' wrists to keep the cuffs from cutting into the skin. Cuff the players' hands firmly behind their backs and double lock them to keep them from tightening. Let the contestants hold the keys in their teeth. At the signal, players attempt to step through the cuffs to bring their arms in front of them. With their hands in front of them, the contestants may now try to free themselves from the cuffs using the key. The first player to execute a total escape wins.

HULA HOOP ESCAPE

Materials:
You will need two large hula hoops for this contest.

The Challenge:
Choose an equal number of players from each team, as many as necessary to tightly stuff one hula hoop held at waist level. Place the other hula hoop over the players, just below their shoulders.

At the signal, all the players try to be the first to escape both hula hoops by ducking underneath. The challenge comes when the hula hoops are already so tightly packed that no one can move. There is also strategy involved, since one team may decide to have half their players try to escape while the other half tries to keep opponents in. The winner is the first one to escape both hula hoops.

Or try this variation: the winner is the first team to have all its members escape the hoop. Whichever variation you try, you will find that teens will want to play this one again. Half the fun is seeing how many you can fit in the hoop.

KEYSTONE COPS

Materials:
Most costume and novelty stores will carry Keystone Cop hats or bobby hats and plastic clubs or nightsticks. Purchase one hat and one club for each contestant. Provide each player with half a dozen eggs in a net bag, burlap sack, or potato sack.

The Challenge:
Each player should have a hat and a club with the bag of eggs tied around her or his shoulders or waist. The bags should be tied in the front leaving the eggs over the player's backside. At a signal, players use the soft plastic clubs to crush other players' eggs while maneuvering to guard their own. As players run all over the stage, it looks like a chase scene from an old Keystone Cop movie. The winner is the player who manages to keep one or more eggs intact.

MEDIEVAL RESCUE

Materials:
Split four cheap plastic handcuffs into two equal pieces at the chain to form shackles. Some novelty stores will carry plastic shackles to save you the trouble. Attach the shackles to the wall about

head high so that the arms will hang a comfortable distance apart. When players are cuffed into these shackles, it looks like a medieval dungeon.

Now take a girl's plastic hair band and poke a stick pin through the center of it. You should have a hair band that fits comfortably on the head, with a pin sticking out the top that will pop a balloon. This makes what we call a "pinhead." Place the pinheads on the prisoners' heads. Now fill about 25 opaque black balloons with water and place them in a tub, barrel, or inflatable children's pool. In one or two of the water balloons, hide a key that will fit any of the plastic handcuff shackles.

The Challenge:

Choose your prisoners to be shackled to the wall. Now choose one girl who will try and rescue each prisoner. At the signal, girls run to the tub of black water balloons. Grabbing a balloon, the girls run to where their prisoners are shackled to the wall. They then pop the water balloons on the prisoners' pinhead hair bands. If the key falls out, then they can release their prisoner. If there is no key, the girls return for another water balloon; they can carry only one balloon at a time. If you have hidden more than one key, then allow play to continue to award a second and third place. The first team to release its prisoner wins.

TONIGHT'S MESSAGE: THE GREAT ESCAPE

Scripture: Matthew 27:62-66.

Illustration:

Have one of the boys from the audience volunteer for a demonstration. Ask the volunteer to clasp his hands or wrists together as tight as he can. Bring two more volunteers up. Have each volunteer grab an elbow and pull, to try and break the first volunteer's grip. If the second two volunteers fail, then call up more volunteers to lock arms and pull until his grip is broken. Have the audience give your volunteers a round of applause as they return to their seats.

Introduction:

Just as it was impossible for this boy to hold his grip, it was impossible for death to keep a grip on Jesus because he was totally without sin. The skeptics, the doubters, and the atheists can try to seal up the tomb as tightly as they know how, but the fact remains that Jesus escaped the power of death. This escape from death makes Christ the greatest escape artist that has ever lived.

Focus:

Because Jesus is the greatest escape artist, *we can trust him to escape the greatest snares of this life.*

1. The snare of temptation (1 Corinthians 10:13). Jesus was successful in not giving in to Satan's greatest temptations. As a high priest who was tempted in all manners like we are and yet was without sin, he knows how to keep us from the temptation of sin.

2. The snare of corruption (2 Peter 1:4). This Scripture tells us that God has given us everything we need for life and godliness. He will help us to escape the awful pull of worldliness and evil desires.

3. The snare of death (Romans 8:11). It is through Christ's sacrificial work that we escape the power of death. We also have the promise of his resurrection power in our lives to quicken or make alive these mortal bodies.

Conclusion:

If all the powers of man could not keep him in the tomb; if sin, corruption, and death could not hold him in their grip, then what keeps you now from receiving him into your heart? Don't hold back through doubt, unbelief, or delay. Let Jesus Christ lead you in the great escape from sin, corruption, and death into life evermore!

4. Wild West Night

COSTUMES, PROPS, AND PROMOTION

Costumes: Encourage the teens to dress up in wild West costumes. They could come as cowboys, Indians, miners, gunfighters, gamblers, or settlers. You could also have a contest for the largest cowboy hat, awarding points or cash for the biggest hat.

Props: Center your props on the stage to heighten interest and curiosity as teens enter. If you are using a snack booth, you may want to put an old west sign above it that says, "Slobbering Sam's Saloon." Have teens pay for their snacks at a table under a sign that says, "Dry Creek Bank." Put "Watering Hole" over drinking fountains and "Ye Ole Out House" over the rest room signs. You may want to cue some classic old western tunes to be played during your competitions.

Promotions: Challenge a popular personality in your junior high school, church, or community to a duel at sundown. Get all the teens to talk it up. You may even be able to get the school principal or coach to accept your challenge. This really draws the teens in. If that isn't possible, then challenge one of the pastors on staff or a popular elder or a deacon. Get them to really go along with it by talking it up and coming out in costume. The duel could be the "Egg Blast," "Candle Hats," or a classic duel using white T-shirts and ink blots or squirt guns with disappearing ink.

ARROWHEADS

Materials:

Purchase a gag arrow-through-the-head device from a local toy or novelty store. Stick a sharp hat pin or nail through the center of the headpiece to make an "Arrowhead." Have a different color balloon for each team. Fill several balloons of each color with shaving cream and hang them with kite string from a five-foot-high rope that spans the front of the stage.

The Challenge:

At the signal, players stand under a balloon of their team's color and jump, attempting to pop the balloon using the sharp pin or the arrowhead. Contestants may hold the arrowhead firmly on their heads, but may not touch the balloons with their hands. The first player to pop all the balloons of his or her team's color is the winner.

BELLY UP TO THE BAR

Materials:

You will need one adjustable table, one two-liter bottle of root beer, and two plastic mugs for each team. Adjust the tables so that one end is slightly higher than the other.

The Challenge:

Choose a bartender and a drinker from each team. Position the bartenders at the high end of the tables farthest from the audience. The drinkers stand or are seated at the low end of the table. At a signal, the bartenders begin to fill mugs with root beer and slide them down the table to the drinkers. The drinkers gulp down the soda and slide the mugs back for more. Having two mugs really keeps the game moving. The first drinker to finish two liters of root beer is the winner.

BRONCO BUST'N'

Materials:

You will need to provide hats for each cowboy rider and feather pillows for each Indian girl contestant. Each team will also need a bronco constructed in one of the following manners:

1. Riders sit on a Harrison Horse or Bounce Pony on top of a table or chair.

2. Bales of straw or hay are stacked three high to make a bale bronco that is easy to tip over.

3. Place a three-inch pipe through the center of a 50-gallon drum. Fasten the pipe securely to two sturdy sawhorses using pipe clamps. This suspends the barrel on the pipe between two sawhorses, making a barrel bronco that is difficult to stay on. Provide crash pads or a spotter when using a barrel bronco.

The idea in each case is to make a bronco that is difficult to stay on for more than 60 seconds under the barrage of enemy Indian fire.

The Challenge:

Have a cowboy mount the bronco.

Choose two girls from a different team to be Indians. At a signal, the Indians each grab a feather pillow and try to beat the cowboy off the bronco. Indians only have 60 seconds to knock the cowboy off. No matter who wins, your cowboy is sure to be in for a ride. The winner is the cowboy who is able to stay on the bronco the entire 60 seconds.

CANDLE HATS

Materials:

Make one candle hat for each contestant by taking a cheap straw or felt cowboy hat and sticking a birthday candle in a plastic holder down into the center of the hat. Provide each contestant with a loaded squirt gun, water cannon, or spray bottle. Be sure to have matches or a lighter for this competition.

The Challenge:

Seat players in a circle facing one another. Each player should wear a candle hat and hold his or her squirt gun. Light all the hats as quickly as possible. At a signal, players fire water at their opponents to try and extinguish their candles. A player is pulled out of the competition when his or her candle goes out. The last player with a lit candle hat is the winner.

EGG BLAST SHOWDOWN

Materials:

You will need an eight-foot section of clear tubing approximately an inch and a half in diameter. The tubing may be purchased at a local hardware store. You will also need a small funnel to fit inside the tubing and a dozen or more eggs.

The Challenge:

Have two contestants face each other about three to four feet apart. Have them each hold one end of the clear plastic tubing. While placing the funnel in one end of the tube, pour one or two raw eggs into the tubing. Shake the egg down to the exact center of the tubing. At a signal, players place the tube in their mouths and blow. You will be surprised at how long a showdown can last and at how many times the kids will want to repeat this little contest. The winner is the contestant who is able to force the egg through the other end of the tube. The loser is obvious.

QUICK-DRAW CONTEST

Materials:

You will need a chalkboard, marker board, or large pad of newsprint with writing instruments. Place your board on a tripod or easel in the center of the stage. Prepare two pieces of paper for each team that have the name of an old Western movie, TV show, or song written on them.

The Challenge:

Teams will compete one at a time in a game of picture charades. One person will be chosen to be the drawer. This person draws a title out of a hat and has 15 seconds to prepare. The person drawing is given a signal and now has 90 seconds to draw pictures that will help the team guess the title. The team may all shout out answers at the same time.

If a portion of the answer is guessed, the drawer may write down that word and an appropriate number of blanks to the right and left, representing the remaining number of words in the title. The drawer may encourage the team with the help of body language, but no talking is allowed. A judge should be on hand to help identify correct answers. The team to guess the answer in the least amount of time is the quick-draw winner.

TONIGHT'S MESSAGE: THE GOOD GUYS AND THE BAD GUYS

Introduction:

In the old Westerns it was always easy to tell the good guys from the bad guys. The good guys always wore white and the bad guys wore black. You also knew that, no matter what terrible things happened during the movie, the good guy would still come out on top.

Today, in these times of increasing moral failure, it is getting harder and harder to tell the good guys from the bad guys. The Bible tells us that there will be false prophets and false motives among those that preach in the last days.

Focus:

Tonight we are going to give you *three ways to tell the good guys from the bad guys.*

1. You will know them by their fruit (Matthew 7:16). You can recognize the good guys because they have the fruit of character and the fruit of good works. The one who is a child of God will act like Jesus. A tree that has bad fruit also has a bad root.

2. You will know them because they preach the Word (Acts 20:29-32). In Paul's farewell to the Ephesians, he warns them that people will come who would try to distort the truth. He warns them to be on their guard and then commits them to the Word of God. The good guys are the ones who will preach the Word as it is, not distorting it for their own purposes.

3. You will know them by their Christ centeredness (1 John 2:22-24). Everything that a godly man does points to Christ. The good guys don't point to themselves, to their church, or to their denomination. They point to Christ our Savior. Beware of those that always draw attention to themselves.

Conclusion:

We have given you tonight three ways to identify the good guys. But what about you? It is dangerous to apply standards to everyone else that you will not apply to yourself. Using these standards from God's Word, which category do you fit into? Are you a good guy or a bad guy? Do you manifest the fruit of Christ in character and good works? Do you accept what the Word says or do you twist or ignore portions that make you uncomfortable? Do you seek in your life to draw attention to Christ and not to yourself? Tonight Christ can make you a good guy! And just like in the old movies, we can know that no matter what happens along the way, we will triumph in the end!

5. A Blast from the Past

COSTUMES, PROPS, AND PROMOTION

Costumes: This is a great night to hold a "come as you were" party. Teens can dress up like babies or small children or just bring baby items like toys, rattles, or teddy bears.

Props: Most stores that carry posters will have a wide selection of baby posters with some great slogans on them. Choose a few of your favorites and hang them on the wall behind your stage. Remember to place all your game props on stage to heighten interest as teens enter. You may want to round up some special songs to play during your game competition, like Amy Grant's "Fat Little Baby."

Promotions: From time to time, you may want to offer incentives to keep your attendance up. "A Blast from the Past" offers a great opportunity for a giant teddy bear giveaway to the person who brings the most visitors. Remind teens to bring a vehicle to enter in the "Baby Races" like a wagon, tricycle, Big Wheel, or baby buggy. You may also want to have an incentive for the winner of this race, such as a trophy or a cash prize.

BABY FOOD FEED

Materials:

Each team will need one jar of baby fruit or dessert, a baby spoon, and a plastic bib.

The Challenge:

Choose two volunteers from each team who won't mind getting a little messy. Have players lie head-to-head on the floor. One player will wear the bib and the other player will serve the baby food. At a signal, the servers will take a spoonful of baby food over their heads and try to get it into the mouths of their partners. Both contestants must keep their heads flat on the floor, and the contestant wearing the bib must keep both hands on the floor. The first team to finish off the jar is the winner.

BABY RACES

Materials:

Encourage the teens in advance to bring a baby vehicle from home. The vehicle can be a peddle car, Big Wheel, tricycle, wagon, or a baby buggy. Each vehicle must be propelled by the rider. No motor-propelled or partner-propelled vehicles are allowed.

The Challenge:

Mark out a course for your baby race. Divide your contestants into heats of four to six racers. The winner of each heat will compete in the final champion's competition. Award the champion team points and a suitable prize or incentive.

BOTTLE BELCH RELAY

Materials:

Each team will need one baby bottle filled with four ounces of Coke or Pepsi. Puncture the nipple of the baby bottle with a clean nail to cause it to flow more freely. Giant baby bonnets will also really add humor to this game.

The Challenge:

Choose a girl to be the mother and a boy to be the baby. Seat girls in folding chairs and have the boys sit on their laps. At the signal, mothers will feed the babies the entire contents of the bottle. When the bottle is empty, mothers lean the babies over their shoulders and pat their backs until they produce a loud belch. The first team to finish the bottle with a loud belch wins.

MAKE ME LAUGH

Materials:

Have several in-house comedians from your youth group or from your sponsor core prepare for this event with funny costumes, faces, monologues, or routines.

The Challenge:

Prepare the audience by saying something along these lines: "It is amazing what people will do to try and entertain a baby. Even the most reserved people will make total fools of themselves. Tough guys will 'goo' and 'coo' just to get a baby to smile. That is the object of our competition this evening."

Choose one volunteer from each team. This volunteer contestant should be a person with a good smile and a good sense of humor. Have the volunteer sit in a chair facing the audience. At the signal, each of three comedians will have 90 seconds to get the contestant to laugh, smile, or show his or her teeth. Comedians are not allowed to touch the contestant.

Each team contestant will face three comedians. The contestant to last the longest without cracking a smile or showing any teeth is the winner.

MOTHER'S REVENGE

Materials:

Supply each team with a large jar of strained baby food, a plastic bib, and a flexible plastic spoon. You may want to prepare for extra mess by putting down additional tarps or sheets of plastic.

The Challenge:

Prepare the audience with a short introduction along these lines: "If you have ever seen a mother trying to feed a baby, you will appreciate this game. Babies usually throw, spit, spill, or drool most of their food all over dear old mom. That is why we present you tonight with Mother's Revenge."

Choose two contestants from each team who won't mind getting messy. Players should face one another in folding chairs about six feet apart. Decide who will be the mother and who will be the baby. If a boy is chosen to be the mother, put a wig on him to add to the humor. Babies will wear the plastic bibs.

At the signal, the mothers take a spoonful of food, draw back on the tip of the spoon, and try to fling it all over their babies. The goal is not to eat the food, but just to plaster your partner. The first team to empty its jar one spoonful at a time is the winner.

WIPE OUT

Materials:

You will need one 40-count tub of baby wipes for each team.

The Challenge:

Place one tub of wipes on the stage in front of each team. Up to 40 members per team can participate in this relay contest. At the signal, each team sends up one player to swipe a wipe and run back to the team. When players get back to their team, another player makes a run for a baby wipe. Play continues until all the wipes are gone. The first team to wipe out is the winner.

The format of the game can be varied by having team members crawl or ride a tricycle up to swipe their wipe. This version takes a little longer, but the results are hilarious. You also may want to find a copy of the 1960s song "Wipe Out" to play during this competition. This adds to the fun!

TONIGHT'S MESSAGE: A CHILD OF GOD

Scripture: 1 John 3:1-10.

Introduction:

Most teens are very insecure about whether they are truly God's children or not. The Bible says that God's Spirit will testify with our spirit that we are God's children (Romans 8:16).

Focus:

Tonight we want to ask *what are the marks of a child of God?*

1. A child of God is born of God (1 John 3:9). There are no grandchildren in the kingdom of God; there are only sons and daughters. That means that no one can trust in their parents' relationship with God, their upbringing, or their heritage. That was the mistake of the Pharisees (Matthew 3:9). Each of us must be born of God. We must be born again into a personal relationship with Jesus Christ.

2. A child of God is obedient (1 John 3:10). The child of God does what is right whether it helps her or his situation or not. Sometimes we lie or cheat or steal because it appears to make things easier on us. That is not true. It is always best to do what is right. A child of God always does what is right because it is the right thing to do. We show our love for the Father by obedience to the Father.

3. A child of God is loving (1 John 3:10). It isn't very popular to love others today. Most people would rather put down, backbite, and slander others. Loving others is what really shows that we are different. It shows that the Gospel is true and that we are truly the children of God.

Conclusion:

Tonight you know whether you are really a child of God or not. We can see that the Spirit will give us that inner confidence that we are God's children. We can also see that there must be outward evidence of that inner change. What keeps you tonight from becoming his child? Don't delay any longer!

6. Pirate Night

COSTUMES, PROPS, AND PROMOTION

Costumes: Invite teens to dress up like their favorite pirate. Suggest things like eye patches, peg legs, pirate hats, hooks, beards, and fake parrots. You can also award bonus points for Jolly Roger flags, T-shirts, or other items that brandish the international pirate symbol.

Props: We will give you an extra hint: Pirate hats can be donated by a Long John Silver's or another local seafood restaurant. These hats are the paper kind that they give away to children, but they will fit teens as well. You can probably get them to donate enough hats for your entire group if you give them enough warning. Also eye patches can be made with black construction paper and a rubber band. This is a very inexpensive way to make pirates out of your whole group and to provide adequate costumes for your games.

You may want to take a king-size sheet and place the skull and crossbones (Jolly Roger) symbol on it using paint, markers, or construction paper. This will make a great pirate backdrop behind your stage. Also, remember to put all game props on the stage in advance to increase interest as teens enter.

Promotions: Our Pirate Night theme was "Hilarious High Seas Adventure." Let the teens know in advance that you will have pirate fights, pirate rescues, and some uncommonly gross contests!

BLUEBEARD BUSTER

Materials:

Purchase some blue soap foam from your local toy store. This item goes by different names, but most stores carry some kind of tub foam that is a colored soap for children. If tub foam is unavailable, you can use ordinary shaving cream. Each team will also need a high-powered squirt gun, squirt bottle, or water cannon.

The Challenge:

Choose two volunteers from each team. One volunteer will be suited in pirate hat, patch, and his or her face will be covered with blue soap foam to form a thick blue beard. The other player is equipped with the water device. Have your Bluebeard stand about six feet from the Buster. At a signal, the Busters open fire on the Bluebeards. The first Buster to spray off his or her pirate's beard is the winner.

CAP'N CRUNCH EAT

Materials:

You will need one box of Cap'n Crunch cereal for every two contestants. Also, supply each contestant with a pirate hat, eye patch, a large mixing bowl, and a huge serving spoon. You will need about a gallon of fresh milk.

The Challenge:

Seat players in pirate costume at a table. Each player gets half a box of Cap'n Crunch cereal in his or her bowl. Pour on the milk and give the signal to start. With the costumes and the rushed table manners, you will be convinced that these guys really are pirates. The first pirate to finish the cereal or the pirate to have eaten the most at the end of one song is the winner.

FOILED AGAIN

Materials:

You will need a four-foot section of heavy-duty aluminum wrap for each contestant. Prepare four shaving cream balloons for each team, assigning each team a different color balloon. Shaving cream balloons can be prepared using ordinary eight- to ten-inch balloons. Fill the balloons three-fourths full of air. Fit the lip of each balloon tightly over a can of nonmenthol shaving foam and push on the nozzle until the balloon is fully inflated. Tie off the balloons and suspend them from a rope spanning the front of the stage.

The Challenge:

Sword fights are an important part of any pirate adventure. Choose a contestant from each team to come forward and make a sword out of the aluminum foil. You may want to award points for the best-looking sword. When all the pirates have made their swords, signal the competition to begin. Pirates rush for the shaving cream balloons of their team's color and attempt to pop them using only their swords. The first pirate to pop all four shaving cream balloons of his or her team's color wins.

FOUR HO HO'S AND A PACKAGE OF GUM

Materials:

Each player will need a pirate's costume, four wrapped Ho Ho's, and a package of chocolate-flavored gum.

The Challenge:

This game is a pun working off the pirate phrase, "Yo ho ho and a bottle of rum!" At a signal, pirates rip into the Ho Ho's and eat them as quickly as possible.

When the Ho Ho's are gone, they begin to chew the entire package of gum. Since the Ho Ho's are still usually stuck to their teeth, the results can be rather hilarious and definitely gross. Have drinking water ready for the contestants after the competition. The first pirate to down the four Ho Ho's, chew the gum, and blow a bubble is the winner.

PIRATE RESCUE

Materials:

Preparation for this game can be handled in one of two ways.

Option 1: Suspend two ropes from your ceiling that are strong enough and sturdy enough to swing on. Beneath the ropes place two or more inflatable baby pools filled with water, shaving cream, or your favorite slime.

Option 2: Place two sturdy nonfolding chairs on either side of the inflatable pools. In this play option, contestants jump from chair to chair rather than swinging across the pools.

The Challenge:

Choose four players from each team. One player is the pirate and the other three are prisoners. The idea of the game is that three prisoners have been taken to an enemy ship. The pirates will swing or jump across from their ships to the enemy ship to rescue the prisoners.

Have the pirates, wearing pirate hats and eye patches, stand on one side of the pools, while the prisoners stand on the other. At a signal, the pirate swings or jumps across to the other ship. When the pirate arrives safely on the other side, the prisoners may swing or jump back to their team's ship one at a time. Any players who fall or drag their feet in a pool must return to the other side and try again. When all three prisoners are safely across, the pirate again crosses to his or her own ship. The first pirate to deliver all players back to his or her own ship is the winner.

POLLY WANT A CRACKER?

Materials:

You will need a balloon, ten soda crackers, and a snorkel for each player. Prepare the snorkels by removing the rubber ring that is found at the top of most snorkels. Then attach the largest balloon you can find to the top of the snorkel. Then replace the ring to form an air-tight seal between the balloon and snorkel. If your snorkels do not have this ring, then you may use a double-wrapped rubber band to attach the balloon.

The Challenge:

Every pirate needs a parrot and every parrot needs a cracker. The object of this game is to eat the crackers and then inflate the balloon through the snorkel until it explodes. You may want to provide extra eye protection, such as safety goggles or sunglasses. The winner is the first contestant to swallow all the crackers and inflate the balloon until it explodes.

TONIGHT'S MESSAGE: A PIRATE'S GREATEST DANGER

Scripture: 1 Timothy 1:18-19.

Introduction:

Pirates faced many dangers on the open seas. Since a pirate's life depended on a ship, the greatest danger was that of shipwreck. This can also be the Christian's greatest danger. In this passage,

Paul talks about those who have shipwrecked their faith. Since the Bible tells us that without faith it is impossible to please God, this is perhaps the Christian's greatest danger.

Focus:

Tonight we are going to share *three things that cause spiritual shipwreck.*

1. We shipwreck our faith when we fail to follow instructions (1 Timothy 1:18). Our faith is undermined when we live in disobedience to the Word of God. Many portions of Scripture warn of the dangers of hearing, believing, or knowing the Word, but not doing what it says (James 1:22; Matthew 7:26).

2. We shipwreck our faith when we do not hold onto that faith (1 Timothy 1:19). The Devil would like nothing better than to cause us to waiver in his faith. The Bible tells us that when a person waivers in his faith, it is like "a wave of the sea, blown and tossed by the wind. That man should not think he will receive anything from the Lord; he is a double-minded man, unstable in all he does" (James 1:6-8).

3. We shipwreck our faith when we do not conduct ourselves in good conscience (1 Timothy 1:19). When we let our standards begin to slip, we are in trouble. First John 3:18-22 tells us that we receive anything we ask from God when our hearts do not condemn us. It is hard to pray and maintain your faith when you are acting contrary to the inner voice of conscience.

Conclusion:

Paul tells us that to reject instruction, faith, and good conscience results in shipwrecked faith. It is not always an obvious event when these things happen. Often these failures are like a coral reef hiding just below the surface. The waters may look blue and safe, but shipwreck is soon to come. We must live in obedience to God's Word, hold to our faith in the Lord Jesus Christ without wavering, and respond to our conscience with conviction. Are you in fear of shipwreck or are you already in a state of shipwreck tonight? Remember that Christ is our Savior, our rescuer, and our anchor in the storm. Come to the Lord Jesus now!

7. The Jell-O Bowl

COSTUMES, PROPS, AND PROMOTION

Costumes: Obviously Jell-O costumes are few and far between, so invite your teens to come dressed in their team color or in the color of their favorite flavor of Jell-O. Encourage them to get creative in arriving covered in color from head to toe. Don't be surprised if teens take you literally.

Props: Since you will be using a huge quantity of Jell-O for this game night, it is a good idea to get some help in the preparation. A few days ahead of time, ask several sponsors or parents to each prepare Jell-O for different game competitions. With several people helping, there will be sufficient preparation time and adequate refrigerator space.

Purchase the Jell-O packages that serve 35 from a large grocery discount store or wholesale warehouse. This will significantly cut your total cost for Jell-O supplies for the night.

Promotions: We have found that everyone loves Jell-O. If they don't like to eat it, chances are they have always wanted to throw it. Inform the teens that the evening will involve everything from eating Jell-O, to throwing it, to squashing it between their toes. You will probably find that this is all the promotion you need. Remind teens also to "Dress for the mess!"

HUMAN JELL-O MAKER

Materials:
You will need one package of presweetened Kool-Aid, along with one cup of warm and one cup of cold water for each contestant. Each person will also need a hula hoop or jump rope.

The Challenge:
Announce to the crowd, "Before you can eat Jell-O, you must make Jell-O. Of course, everyone knows that Jell-O is easy to make. You just combine the Jell-O mix with hot and cold water and mix it up well. Tonight we are going to accomplish this process in human blenders."

Call up your volunteers. At a signal, contestants swallow the Jell-O mix (presweetened Kool-Aid) and then drink one cup of warm and one cup of cold water. They must then hula hoop or jump rope ten times to mix the ingredients. The first person to fully blend his or her ingredients is the winner.

JELL-O GUZZLE

Materials:
Each player will need a Jell-O guzzler. The Jell-O guzzlers are made by filling empty two-liter soft drink containers with liquid Jell-O and placing them in the refrigerator until the Jell-O is solid.

The Challenge:
In this contest, each player must consume all of the Jell-O in a two-liter container. Players may shake it, squeeze it, jiggle it, or suck out the Jell-O. The first person to guzzle all the Jell-O from a container is the winner.

JELL-O JAM

Materials:
Each contestant will need one large bowl of Jell-O and an empty eight-ounce Coke bottle.

The Challenge:
Seat contestants at a table with their own Coke bottle and bowl of Jell-O. At a signal, players will pick up the Jell-O and

try to jam it into the Coke bottles. No pouring is allowed, but players may put the Jell-O in their mouths and spit it back into the bottles. The first person to fully jam a bottle with Jell-O is the winner.

JELL-O SLURP'N'

Materials:

Equip each contestant with a bowl of Jell-O and a straw.

The Challenge:

At a signal, contestants will begin to slurp up the Jell-O through the straw. The first person to finish off the bowl is the winner.

If you like to do things big, then prepare a large tub of Jell-O and provide several straws for each team. Choose three volunteers from each team to try and slurp up the entire tub of Jell-O. The first team to succeed, or the last team to pass out and turn blue, is the winner.

JELL-O TOSS

Materials:

Prepare ten to 12 Jell-O bombs for each team. The Jell-O bombs can be made using regular water balloons, a large amount of liquid Jell-O, and a water balloon pump. Water balloon pumps or fillers are available at most toy stores. Fill the water balloon pump with liquid Jell-O. Fill and tie the balloons. Put the filled balloons in the refrigerator to solidify. When the Jell-O has set, pop the balloons. Small hand-sized Jell-O bombs or grenades are the result.

If your store does not carry a water balloon pump or filler, then you can use an empty container of dishwashing liquid. Fill the container with liquid Jell-O. Fit the balloon over the lip of the container and squeeze the bottle to fill. Tie the filled balloons and refrigerate.

Each team will also need a net bag, shopping bag, or beach bag. The bag needs to have looped handles that are large enough to fit over a teen's head.

The Challenge:

Choose three volunteers who are dressed for the mess. One volunteer will be the tosser and the other two will be catchers. Have the catchers each place one looped handle of the net bag over their heads so that the bag is suspended between them.

At a signal, the tossers grab Jell-O bombs and throw them to their teammates. Catchers run underneath the Jell-O bomb and try to catch it in their net bag. This game is hilarious since most of the Jell-O ends up on the catchers' heads.

The team to catch the most Jell-O bombs is the winner.

TOE JAM

Materials:

Prepare two sets of tubs or cake pans filled with cubed Jell-O. Place five large marbles at the bottom of each tub.

The Challenge:

You guessed it! Contestants must attempt to remove the marbles with their toes. Have contestants take off their shoes and socks. Seat them in folding chairs facing the audience and place one tub of Jell-O at the feet of each contestant. At a signal, players work to remove all five marbles using only their bare feet. The first player to remove all five marbles wins.

TONIGHT'S MESSAGE: WHAT'S SHAPING YOU?

Scripture: Romans 12:1-2.

Introduction:

Jell-O will take whatever shape you mold it into. We saw that demonstrated tonight by putting Jell-O into some shapes you have probably never seen before. Christians are like that. We will be whatever we let ourselves to be molded into. One translation (Phillips) interprets this Scripture as, "Don't let the world around you squeeze you into its own mold. . . ." There are many things that will try and mold our lives and keep us from being holy and pleasing to God.

Focus:

Tonight we want to look at some of the *molds that shape people's lives.*

1. The mold of peer pressure. I think one of the worst cases of peer pressure I know is that of Pilate. He knew that Jesus was innocent and wanted to release him, but because he feared the crowd, he released Christ to be crucified (Luke 23:20-25). Peer pressure is one of the most dangerous molds the world has to offer. If we are squeezed into a mold by public opinion, we may never stand for Christ.

2. The mold of tradition. Jesus was constantly battling with people's tradition (Matthew 15:6). Our preconceived ideas of what life is supposed to be can prevent us from experiencing the abundant life God intended for us in Christ Jesus. "We've never done it that way," has killed more revival and renewal movements than any other foe.

3. The mold of the media. Sometimes we forget that the media present us with only a fantasy world. Statistics say that by the time teenagers are 18, they will have been exposed to some 60,000 hours of media, 10,000 hours of school, and considerably fewer hours of religious training. If we are not watchful, it will be easy for this entire generation to be squeezed into the materialistic, immoral mold that today's media present.

4. The mold of a true Christian. Romans 8:29 says that God is conforming us "to the likeness of his Son. . . ." That means that while all the world is trying to shape us into a false image, God is busy making us more like Jesus. When we place our lives in God's hands, he will mold us and shape us like a master potter.

God commands in the Law that no image or idol be made of him. Perhaps that is because he himself is preparing us to be the very image of his dear Son.

Conclusion:

The Christian is like Jell-O. You will take the shape of whatever mold you are fit into. That is not to say that you will be a product of your environment, but that you can choose today what influences and powers will mold and shape your life for eternity.

8. Fire Fighter Follies

COSTUMES, PROPS, AND PROMOTION

Costumes: Invite teens to come dressed as fire fighters or fire victims. Some teens will come with charcoal rubbed all over their faces, others in bandages. Encourage the teens to use their imaginations for this one. One of our teens talked the fire chief into bringing a fire truck over and got bonus team points.

Props: Have some of your more artistic teens paint a mural that can be hung behind the stage. The mural might be a humorous portrayal of fire fighter follies, or a serious picture of a raging fire. Remember to set out all of the game props before the teens arrive. This will help arouse curiosity and interest.

Promotions: The very theme of Fire Fighter Follies lends itself to all kinds of promotion tactics. There are great slogans like "Beat the Heat with the . . ." or you might make posters and flyers showing fire fighters jumping from a high building, with the caption "Don't Miss This!"

BLANKET RESCUE

Materials:

Each team will need one blanket, four strong boys, and several brave girls.

The Challenge:

Place the girls at the front of the auditorium and the boys at the back. At a signal, the boys will race to the front. Each boy holds one corner of the blanket and one girl climbs into the center of the blanket. The boys then race the girl to the back of the auditorium. Play continues until all of the girls have been rescued. The first team to transport all its girls safely to the back of the auditorium wins.

BUCKET BRIGADE

Materials:

You will need five small buckets or plastic cups for each team. Each team will also need one large bucket of water and one empty medium-sized bucket.

The Challenge:

Get five volunteers from each team and form one line for each team, with the volunteers lining up one behind the other. At the front of each line, place the empty bucket. At the back of the line, place the large bucket of water. Then give each player one of the small buckets.

At a signal, the back players will fill their buckets. The players directly in front of them will place their buckets over their heads to be filled by the back players. The water is passed up the line in this manner until the front players dump the water into the medium-sized buckets. Only the back players may turn around; all other players must face the front during this competition. The first team to fill the front bucket wins.

CANDLE HATS

Materials:

This game is a favorite repeated from the Wild West Night's "Candle Hats" competition. Here you will probably want to use a different style of hat. Fire-fighter helmets are available at local toy stores. Arm each contestant with a squirt gun or squirt bottle and a candle hat.

The Challenge:

Seat players in a circle facing one another. Light all the candle hats and give each contestant a squirt gun. At a signal, players and challengers open fire. When a candle goes out, that player is pulled out, while play continues for the other contestants. The person with the last hat still lit is the winner.

A variation of this game uses two contestants from each team. One team member is the fire fighter, the other is the fire bug. The fire fighters wear fire hats and have the squirt guns. The fire bugs wear candle hats and are seated at least five feet from the fire fighters. Once everyone is in position, the candle hats are lit and the fire fighters are blindfolded. At a signal, the fire fighters try to extinguish their team's candle hat. The first team to put out the fire is the winner.

CHILI-EATING CONTEST

Materials:

Each contestant will need a large plate of chili dogs.

The Challenge:

Fire fighters are famous for their chili cook-offs—to see who can make the hottest or the best chili. In this case, it's a contest to find the fastest chili-eating fire fighter. Seat contestants at a table with a large plate of chili dogs in front of each person. At a signal, players eat the chili dogs, but without using their hands. The first contestant to finish the chili dogs is the winner.

You can add to the fun by having the contestants wear plastic pig noses or by secretly adding a little hot sauce or a hot pepper to the chili dogs. You might also choose to have a true hot chili contest as part of the evening's events, with teens bringing their own homemade chili. Any variation you choose is sure to be a big hit.

FIRE DRILLS

Materials:

You will need a plastic fire hat, some rubber boots, oversized pants, and/or fire coats for each contestant. Each contestant will also need a cot or a mat to lie on. A bell, buzzer, or alarm clock starts the contest: the louder the alarm the better.

The Challenge:

Have each contestant, now a fire fighter, lie on a cot or a mat. All the fire clothes (hat, boots, pants) are placed at the foot of the cots or mats. Choose a girl from each team to play the victim and have them all sit at the back of the auditorium. When the alarm sounds, the fire fighters jump up and put their fire clothes on. As soon as they are fully dressed, they leave the stage and run to the back row where they will put the girls over their shoulders and carry them back to the stage. The first fire fighter to bring the team victim safely to the front is the winner.

You may want to run this variation throughout the course of the evening.

Have the fire fighters lie on the cots during the entire program. Whenever the alarm sounds, the fire fighters must go into action. Sound the fire alarm every time the game night gets a little slow. After each drill, the fire fighters must take off all their fire gear and return to their cots. The girls return to their seats and all await the next alarm.

WATER BALL

Materials:

There are two great options for this game, depending on how involved you want to get. In both cases you will need a high-powered squirt gun or water cannon for each contestant. With the first option, you will also need one four-inch styrofoam ball and an orange marker cone for each team. The second option is more involved and will take some special preparation. You must begin by making one water ball for each team.

Water balls can be made by punching a hole through the center of a four-inch styrofoam ball using a pen or pencil. You then place an ordinary drinking straw through the hole so that an inch of the straw sticks out on either side of the ball. Then thread 50 feet of kite string through each of the water balls.

Water balls can now be hung by attaching the string to the walls at the front and the back of your auditorium. Attach the string on the front wall at a height of about eight feet and the string on the back wall at a slightly lower level, put-

ting the string at a slant. Test your water guns to be sure that they have sufficient pressure to move the water balls down the string.

The Challenge:

If playing the first option, place the styrofoam balls on the orange marker cones, positioning one in front of each team. Equip each team player with a high-powered squirt gun or water cannon. At the signal, players will try to blast the ball off the cone using the water pressure. The first team to knock off the ball wins.

With the second option, you start the water balls about ten feet from the front wall. Choose one contestant from each team to be the fire fighter. Arm each player with a water gun and give the signal. As players shoot the water ball, it should slide toward the back of the auditorium. While the ball slides down the string, the teams are getting soaked. The first player to reach the back of his or her team with the water ball is the winner.

TONIGHT'S MESSAGE: FIRE FIGHTERS

Introduction:
Every day in America, fire fighters go out to battle fires knowing that, if one gets out of control, it could be a matter of life or death. Teenagers face the same danger today in dealing with fires of a different kind.

Focus:
Tonight we will speak about *three fires that every teen must fight.*

1. The fire of the tongue (James 3:5-6). If you have ever had a lie get out of control, then you know how the tongue is like a fire. Today it is so popular to cut others down, to slander, and to lie. Proverbs 26:18-19 shows us that even our joking around can be deadly. Every teen must guard against the fire of the tongue by committing that member of his or her body to serving only God's purposes in encouraging and building up.

2. The fire of passion (Proverbs 6:23-29). The fires of passion are raging hot in America today. This passage warns us that you cannot put fire in your lap without getting burned. Passion will receive its payment. Control your passions by not adding fuel to the fire. Keep your eyes and ears from media that would kindle the flames of passion in your heart. God has reserved those fires for marriage. The Song of Solomon warns us over and over not to arouse or awaken love before it is time. We need to heed this warning to guard against the destructive force of unbridled passion.

3. The fire of judgment (Revelation 20:15). Every person will face the fires of judgment. For Christians, we know that only their works will be tested by fire. For those without a personal relationship with Jesus, their whole lives will be consumed in fire. The everlasting fires of hell will be their final judgment. We can fight this fire by living and preaching the Gospel. Jude 23 tells us that it is our responsibility to snatch others from the fire. What if your house caught on fire and you escaped, but your family and friends were still inside? How could you live with yourself if you didn't try to help? It is our responsibility in love to keep ourselves and our neighbors from the judgment to come.

Conclusion:
Fire is a dangerous thing. Let no one think that he or she can toy with just a little fire without it getting out of control. Fight fire with fire. Get on fire for God and let your tongue and your passion honor him and you will never fear the fires of judgment!

9. The Snow Blast

COSTUMES, PROPS, AND PROMOTION

Costumes: Invite teens to come out in all sorts of winter clothes. Hats, scarves, ski clothes, and winter coats would all be appropriate. Teens can also bring sleds, skis, or skates for bonus team points.

Props: Line the wall behind your stage with sleds, skis, and toboggans. This will get everyone in the winter spirit. You may also want to make some large snow-flakes by folding and cutting white construction paper. These can be taped to the walls or hung with string all over your auditorium to achieve that "winter wonderland" look. Remember to place all game props out on stage before the program begins to increase interest as teens are arriving.

Promotions: The Snow Blast is a great

event any time of year. You may want to hold this event in the summer and advertise, "Beat the Heat at the Snow Blast!" The event also works great in late fall, advertised as "A Warm-Up for Winter Fun!" If you hold your Snow Blast in winter, then you may want to give away tickets to a winter festival or sporting event. Tickets to a local ice skating rink could also be given away to the person who brings the most visitors. As spring approaches, you may want to have the Snow Blast as a "Farewell to Winter Party!" This also works well when the winter season has offered a limited snowfall. The Snow Blast can serve as an indoor event to compensate for a bad ski trip. You can bill it as "The Last Blast!"

FROSTING THE SNOWMAN

Materials:

Provide each team with one can of white frosting and some different colored candies. Also provide each team with a soft plastic spoon or knife.

The Challenge:

Choose one boy and two girls from each team. Have the boys sit in folding chairs. At a signal, the boys lean their heads back and the girls begin to decorate their faces with white frosting and candies. The object is to create the best looking snowman. This is more of a contest than a race, so allow at least three or more minutes for the girls to be creative. Once they finish, the girls present their creations to the audience. Let crowd response determine the winner. You may want to play "Frosty the Snowman" over your PA system during this competition.

ICE SKATING

Materials:

Make a pair of indoor ice skates for each contestant. The skates are made using two ice trays with removable dividers. Take out the dividers and fill the trays with water. If trays are unavailable, then use small disposable cake pans. Place long shoe laces across the ice tray so that the center of the laces will freeze inside the ice. Leave the tips of the laces hanging out and freeze the trays with the laces in them. When the water freezes solid, you will have a pair of indoor ice skates that can be tied to the bottoms of tennis shoes.

The Challenge:

Call for volunteers from each team. Allow the contestants to sit in folding chairs to tie their ice skates to their shoes. Make sure the laces are tied snugly enough to hold the skates onto the shoes. Mark out a course using tape or marker cones on a concrete, tile, or tarp-covered surface.

At a signal, contestants will race to a finish line. These skates are so slick that it offers a great challenge to get to a finish line even a short distance away. The results are hilarious. The first racer to cross the finish line is the winner.

INDOOR SNOW SKI SAFARI

Materials:

This game is for those wild and creative gamesters who are willing to go the distance and do something out of the ordinary. The preparation is a bit involved, but the excitement this event generates is well worth the trouble. You will need to make a pair of skis for each team and one sledding slope. You will also need a plastic sled for each team.

Use a 1" x 4" x 6' board for each ski. Make three "foot loops" on each ski using pieces of rope or cord. Attach the loops to each side of the board with a loop large enough for a foot to slip through. Space the loops about 16 inches apart with one at the midpoint of the six-foot ski. You will need two skis for each team.

To make a sledding ramp, purchase a 4' x 12' sheet of one-inch thick plywood and some two-by-fours for reinforcement. You can start the ramp at the top of your stage and have it going to the floor, or set up two sturdy tables to support the ramp, slanting it to the stage floor. Cover the ramp with a thick plastic tarp or a disposable paint cloth. Tape the plastic to the ramp using duct tape and cover the ramp with Vaseline to make it slick.

Provide each team with a pair of skis and one plastic sled. Now get ready for a wild and exciting competition.

The Challenge:

Announce that this competition will be a combination relay using team cross-country skiing and a sled race down the dreaded slick mountain slope. Choose four contestants from each team. Three teammates will climb into the skis. The fourth team member will ride the sled. Have all contestants line up at a starting line with the sled riders in front of the skiers. At a signal, the sledders will race to the slick slope and slide down on their plastic sleds. At the bottom of the slope, they will return to the starting line to tag their team skiers. The skiers will then shuffle their way, making one lap around their team. When they complete their lap, they will tag their sledder, who will perform one more daring slide down the slope. The first team back to the finish line is the winner.

You may want to expand this game and have several groups of skiers and several sledders tag off in an extended relay of skiing and sledding. Plan the relay so that the final leg of the race is on a sled. The team whose final sled rider crosses the finish line first is the winner.

SNO BALL-EATING CONTEST

Materials:

One of the well-known snack cake companies makes a pink coconut-covered cake called a Sno Ball. Purchase three packages of Sno Balls (two per package) for each contestant. Don't forget to check with the day-old bakery for a bargain.

The Challenge:

Seat contestants at a table and have them put their hands behind their backs. If you want, you can have the contestants wear winter hats. Stack six Sno Balls on a paper plate in front of each contestant. At a signal, contestants eat the Sno Balls without using their hands. The first person to finish a plate of Sno Balls is the winner.

SNOWBALL FIGHT

Materials:

Fill several large garbage bags full of wadded newspaper or white bond paper. Mark your stage area into equal sections for each team using colored tape to create floor boundaries.

The Challenge:

Choose several players from each team to defend their team's boundaries from the advancing blizzard. Players must stay inside their own boundaries at all times. Dump out the bags of wadded paper so that they are spread evenly between the teams.

At a signal, players try to clear their area of the wadded paper snowballs. Players may kick, scoot, or throw the snowballs. Each team frantically attempts to clear its area by heaping the paper snowballs into another team's territory. The result looks like a giant indoor snowball fight. Allow about three minutes per game. At the end of three minutes, judge which area is most free of snow and award a winner. You may want to pick a new set of team players and go for another round.

WILD WINTER WARM-UP

Materials:

Go to a flea market, garage sale, or discount store to buy some oversized pants and some large boots and mittens. Purchase an equal number of winter items for each team. You may also be able to gather these items from your church members.

The Challenge:

Establish a course around your auditorium. You may want to have players race around their teams. Choose four runners from each team. Line the runners up in relay fashion. At a signal, the first runners will dress in the winter warm-up clothes and race around their teams. When they complete one lap, they take off the clothes and the next runner puts on the garments to complete the next lap. Since all the garments are oversized, it is hilarious to watch the runners try to keep all the clothes on. The first team's runners to complete all their laps and cross the finish line with all their clothes still on is the winner.

TONIGHT'S MESSAGE: WHITER THAN SNOW

Scripture: Psalm 51:7.

Introduction:

There is nothing quite as pure and fresh looking as the first snow of the year as it covers the stripped branches of a stately oak tree. There is nothing quite so beautiful. It is no wonder then that God uses this as a symbol for what he can do in the life of any sinner who repents and turns his heart toward him.

Focus:

Tonight we want to share with you the *three "C's" of God's forgiveness* that make a Christian white as snow.

1. He covers our sin. As the snow covers the bleak ground of winter with a white blanket, so does God cover us with Christ's blood, a blanket of forgiveness. Like a typing error that must be whited out so that the correct mark can be put in its place, God's covering of our sins is just the first step to fulfilling his purpose in our lives.

2. He cleanses our heart. God is the only one who can take a person's heart that has been blackened by sin, wash it in his crimson blood, and have it come out whiter than snow. God cleanses our hearts and our consciences from the stain of all past sins. He cleanses away the guilt and the judgment that darkens a person's heart and countenance.

3. He creates us anew. God does not leave us alone after we have been covered and cleansed to go back to the world and stain our lives again with sin's dark blot. He creates in us a new heart, a willing and steadfast spirit. As the winter snows cover the ground to prepare it for spring's new life, so does Christ's work of forgiveness prepare us for a new heart. New birth is part of the wondrous glory of the Gospel of Jesus Christ.

Conclusion:

It does not matter what you have done or how great your sin, the Lord will forgive you. But don't settle for just his covering or his cleansing. So many in the world come to Christ for forgiveness but never experience the rebirth that will truly set them free. Let him create in you a new heart tonight!

10. Mexican Fiesta

COSTUMES, PROPS, AND PROMOTION

Costumes: Since any teenager can wrap himself in a blanket and paint on a mustache, that means everyone can come decked out for the Mexican Fiesta. Some students will come wearing sombreros; some of the girls may come in Mexican dresses. Encourage all the teens to participate in this special celebration.

Props: Check with your local party supply store for some Mexican decorations. Hanging piñatas and a variety of colored streamers and balloons will add to the mood of a fiesta. You may want to get some upbeat Mexican music to play during the competitions. Word Records has several contemporary Christian tapes available in Spanish. Do some research at your local Christian bookstore or tape outlet to get one of these.

Promotions: Mexico is widely known in America as a party place or vacation spot. Advertise your fiesta using brightly colored flyers or posters with sayings like "For Fun South of the Border" or "Make a Run for the Border at the Mexican Fiesta." Invite your school Spanish classes.

Have one of your teens sing Sandi Patti's "Via Dolorosa" toward the end of your program as a special event. If you have Mexican missionaries, this would be a great time to generate interest for their work or to have one of them as a guest speaker.

FAKE TEQUILA

Materials:

You will need one bottle of club soda or carbonated spring water for each contestant. Peel off the label and drop a candy "gummy worm" into the bottle just before the game begins.

The Challenge:

Explain to your audience that tequila is a famous party drink in Mexico. It is an alcoholic drink made from a cactus. At the bottom of true tequila, there is a cactus worm that is considered by some to be the prized portion of the bottle. Since we don't condone the drinking of alcoholic beverages, we will use club soda and a gummy worm.

Choose your contestants and have them come up front and face the audience. At a signal, contestants will begin to drink the fake tequila. The object is to drink all the tequila and save the worm for last. If the worm slithers down early, participants should hold it in their hand until all the liquid is consumed. When the bottle is empty, players should hold the worms in their mouths just long enough for the judge and the crowd to see. The first person to down his or her bottle gets the worm and the win.

GUACAMOLE DIP FLIP

Materials:

Each team will need a small bowl of pistachio pudding and a flexible plastic spoon. This pudding looks like guacamole dip, but is much cheaper. You may also want to supply large bibs for the participants who will be on the receiving end of the dip flip.

The Challenge:

Select two contestants from each team. Have them sit about two feet apart in folding chairs. At the signal, players will try to flip the dip one spoonful at a time into their partner's mouth. Have a judge determine the most successful catches and, when all the dip is gone, award a winner.

PIÑATA POP

Materials:

A piñata is a must at any Mexican fiesta. The Mexican piñata was originally a large paper bag filled with nuts and candies wrapped in wax paper. The mouth of the bag is tied and hung from the ceiling with a cord. The bag is decorated with tissue paper or wrapped with streamers.

Prepare one piñata for each team using a brown grocery bag or lunch sack. Fill only one bag with candy and treats. The other bags may hold flour and rice, water balloons, or shaving cream. Have a blindfold and a striking stick for each team. These sticks should be made of plastic or other soft materials. Decorate the outsides of your piñatas with streamers or tissue paper, and suspend them from the ceiling with a cord.

The Challenge:

Choose two volunteers from each team. These players are assigned a piñata by drawing lots or by some alphabetical or birthday order. Have one of the volunteers from each team blindfold and spin the other player on their team around. Hand each blindfolded player a striking stick and send her or him hunting for the team piñata. The volunteers may yell directions and keep their players from striking another player. You may want to inform the players in advance that only one piñata has candy in it, or you can surprise them. The player to burst the piñata full of candy is the winner.

TACO-EATING CONTEST

Materials:

Purchase or prepare several tacos for each contestant. Adding a little extra hot sauce or hot peppers to the taco meat will spice up the contest. Have additional sauce available.

The Challenge:

Send volunteers from each team out of the room to be dressed in Mexican costumes. Costumes can be as simple as a poncho, sombrero, or Mexican mustache. While the players are out of the room, explain to the audience about the added hot sauce. Call the players back into the room and seat them at a table with the tacos and a choice of sauces. Warn the contestants that the tacos may be a little dry and suggest that they will probably want to add a little sauce. When players have prepared their tacos, give the signal for contestants to begin eating. The first player to finish his or her tacos wins the game and a large glass of ice water.

TORTILLA TOSS

Materials:

Have one straw sombrero and a package of 12 flour tortillas for each team.

The Challenge:

Choose two volunteers from each team and position them about eight to ten feet apart. Designate one player to be the catcher; the catcher will wear the sombrero. Tossers will stand with their backs to the catchers.

At a signal, the tossers will begin to throw tortillas over their backs to the catchers. The catchers will run underneath the tortillas to try and catch them in the broad rim of their sombreros. The catchers must keep the sombreros on their heads. The team to catch the most flying tortillas is the winner.

TOSTI-TOES AND CHEESE

Materials:

You will need a new pair of white tube socks, a bowl of tortilla chips, and a small bowl of cheese dip for each team.

The Challenge:

Choose one boy and one girl from each team. The girl should remove her socks and shoes and put on the white tube socks. Have both players sit on the floor facing one another with the bowls of chips and cheese dip between them.

At a signal, the girl will pick up a chip with her toes and dip it in the cheese. While she holds the chip steady, the boy will eat the tosti-toes from her feet. Neither player is allowed to use his or her hands. The girl may use her toes or both feet to pick up and dip the chips. The first team to finish off its bowl of chips is the winner.

TONIGHT'S MESSAGE: FIESTA OR SIESTA?

Introduction:

In case you haven't caught on yet, *fiesta* means a party or celebration. The Mexican people also have a custom where, during the heat of the day, a town will close down for a time of rest until the cooler portion of the afternoon or evening. This is called a *siesta*.

Focus:

Every person here tonight is spiritually heading for a fiesta or siesta. **Which one are you heading for?**

1. The siesta (Romans 13:11-14). Most of the people on this planet are in a state of spiritual slumber. It is as if they have overslept and missed the Good News of Christ's coming. Because they are unaware of his coming, they busy themselves with orgies, drunkenness, sexual immorality, debauchery, dissension, and jealousy. They actually think that the fiesta will be in hell. In their slumber, they don't realize that hell is a place of eternal torment; there are no parties there and no meetings with your friends. The Devil will have no control there. He himself will be under the worst judgment and punishment.

2. The fiesta (Luke 15:10). The Bible tells us that when one sinner repents, all of heaven stops to rejoice. This is preparing us for the biggest celebration of all, that of the wedding supper of the Lamb (Revelation 19:7). On that day, the church will be united with the Lord forever. This is a fiesta to anticipate! It will be joy evermore to be with the Lord in heaven forever!

Conclusion:

Where are you spiritually tonight? Are you asleep to the fact of Christ's coming? Are you like the disciples in the garden who were too sleepy to watch and pray with him in his most crucial hour? Are you asleep to the joy in this life of knowing and serving the Lord? You can begin a fiesta right now by turning to God and repenting of your sins. Even now you can begin to experience the real celebration that comes in knowing Christ Jesus as Lord.

11. Armed Forces Night

COSTUMES, PROPS, AND PROMOTION

Costumes: Encourage teens to come in military uniforms, khakis, or camouflage pants, shirts, and hats. Teens may want to bring *Rambo, Iron Eagle, Platoon*, or other military movie posters from home for bonus team points.

Props: Line the back wall with nets and camouflage. Check with your local army supply store for other costume and prop

ideas. Remember to place all game props on stage in advance to increase teens' interest as they enter the auditorium.

Promotions: Advertise a night where everyone in the building will get to participate. Dave Roever is a youth evangelist and Vietnam war veteran with a great testimony. The group Truth for Youth Military Ministries has put out a color cartoon tract called, "Miracle in Vietnam: The Dave Roever Story." You may want to purchase a large quantity of these by writing Evangelism Literature for America, 1445 Boonville Ave., Springfield, MO 65802. Sow for revival by offering one of these cartoon books to everyone who enters, or as an incentive to the first 100 teens to enter that night. You may also want to purchase a video of Dave's life story as a giveaway, prize, or incentive.

Armed Forces Night could lend itself to a host of guest speakers. Have one of the veterans in your church share a short, exciting testimony with the teens. Check with a local armed service branch for a chaplain who might want to speak to your teens.

AIRPLANE LANDING

Materials:

Supply each person in the auditorium with one piece of paper and a pen or pencil. Place a toy or model aircraft carrier at the front of the room as a target. Other suitable targets could be an army helmet or a regular wastebasket.

The Challenge:

Everyone uses the sheets of paper to design a paper airplane. Have participants write their names on their paper airplanes. At a signal, the audience launches the airplanes at the target. The audience member to land a plane on or nearest the target wins a prize and points for his or her team.

CREAM PIE PUSH-UPS

Materials:

Prepare a cream pie for each contestant by filling an aluminum pie tin with nonmenthol shaving cream. Place a cherry with a stem in the center of each cream pie.

The Challenge:

Choose one athletic male recruit from each team. Have each recruit assume the upper stance of a push-up position. Choose a girl to hold his ankles. While the recruit maintains the up position, place a pie directly under his face. Then ask the recruits to place one hand behind their backs.

At a signal, the recruits will attempt to lower themselves to remove the cherry using only their teeth and without falling into the cream pie. Players may not use their other hands to steady themselves. Girls hold their ankles to keep the recruits from rolling away or from hitting the pie. Recruits that fail will get a face full of shaving cream. The winner is the first player to retrieve the cherry "single-handedly."

Materials:

Construct a mountain similar to the slick slope in the Snow Blast's "Indoor Snow Ski Safari." Place a five-eighths to one-inch 4' x 12' sheet of plywood against the front wall, the stage, or up against two sturdy tables. Make sure the slope is as steep as possible. Support and stabilize the slope for play using two-by-four studs. Cover the plywood with plastic, and tape down the plastic with duct tape. Grease the plastic sheet with Vaseline, baby oil, or other slick, yet washable, substance. Hang a flag or handkerchief four feet above the peak of the incline.

The Challenge:

Choose a volunteer from each team. At a signal, players try to be the first to scale the incline and capture the flag. Play is

complicated by the slick surface, steep incline, and the fact that each player is trying to keep opponents from reaching the top. Be sure to pad the sides of the slope or to have spotters available to catch the slipping and sliding volunteers. The first person to capture the flag is the winner and is declared king of the mountain.

Materials:

Provide each team with one sturdy cot, a table, one roll of toilet paper, and a tube of fake blood or a squirt bottle of ketchup.

The Challenge:

Choose five volunteers from each team. Each team has one doctor, one nurse, and three patients. The patients should be smaller teens who can be carried easily. Each patient will have a different injury: one will have an arm injury, one a leg injury, and one a head injury.

At a signal, the arm-injury patient will jump onto the table and lie down. The doctor squirts the fake blood or ketchup

on the patient's arm and the nurse wraps the wound with a toilet-paper bandage. When the wound has been dressed, the patient jumps onto a cot. Have some strong boys from each team pass the cot to the audience. The team must work together to pass the patient over the heads of the audience to the back of the auditorium.

When a patient reaches the back, he or she is considered rescued. The patient jumps off the cot and the cot is passed back to the front. Meanwhile, the doctor is treating the leg wound and the nurse is dressing it with toilet paper. The leg-injury patient jumps on the cot and is passed to the back, just like the arm-injury patient. Play continues until each casualty patient has been rescued. The first team to treat and rescue all its wounded wins.

MESS HALL MADNESS

Materials:

Prepare trays or plates full of military-type food like beans and hot dogs or sloppy joes. Set up a table with enough chairs for the contestants.

The Challenge:

Choose one contestant from each team to be seated at the table. These recruits place their hands behind their backs. At a signal, recruits are to eat as fast as they can without using their hands. The first one to finish his or her plate is the winner.

SERGEANT SAYS

Materials:

Practice in advance by quickly barking out tricky "Simon Says" commands.

The Challenge:

This game is a twist on "Simon Says." Since sergeants are well known for their abuse of new recruits, the sergeant will insult and try to trick the recruits. Players are to respond quickly to each command that begins with "Sergeant Says. . . ." As the "Sergeant," you try to catch players off guard by calling them names, asking them to do the impossible, and bellowing commands quickly. When a player makes a mistake, she or he must sit down.

When several players have been disqualified, commend the remaining recruits and invite them to spread out a little bit, now that you have more room. If players move, then have them sit down because you didn't say "Sergeant Says" first! This usually catches most of the remaining players. The last player standing is the winner.

TONIGHT'S MESSAGE: LEARN TO FIGHT

Tonight we will identify some *keys to spiritual warfare* using the acrostic, "FIGHT!"

1. F is for Fear the Lord (Proverbs 9:10). To fear the Lord is to have a prop-er attitude toward God. Every soldier must have a proper respect and measure of obedience toward his or her commanding officer.

2. I is for Increase your faith (1 Co-

rinthians 16:13). The soldier of Christ must constantly be on guard, standing firm in the faith. To question or hesitate in obeying the commands of an officer could be a matter of life or death. Soldiers must have faith in their commander's ability to see what is ahead. They must learn absolute trust.

3. G is for Guard your heart (Proverbs 4:23-27). Above all else, soldiers must guard their hearts, for the heart is the wellspring of life. Verses 24 to 27 of this chapter tell us that we may guard our hearts by watching our words, our gaze, and our ways.

4. H is for Hate sin (James 4:4). Friendship with the world is hatred toward God. Soldiers are trained to hate their enemies. We must love what God loves and hate what God hates.

5. T is for Testify (Revelation 12:11). One of the greatest weapons we have as soldiers of Christ is our testimony. Being shod with the preparation of the Gospel of peace shows that our testimony is also part of our defense.

Conclusion:

Using these keys from the word *fight*, we can learn to stand our ground against the Evil One. According to these keys, are you a soldier of Christ? Life is either treated as a battleground or a playground. Are you part of the battle or are you just messing around? Choose today to join the everlasting army in the war against sin, worldliness, death, hell, and the grave by giving your life wholly to the Lord of Hosts!

12.

The Big Barn Blowout

COSTUMES, PROPS, AND PROMOTION

Costumes: Invite the kids to "farm out" for this fun event. Straw hats, overalls, painted freckles, and blacked-out teeth can all add to the *Hee-Haw* humor of the evening. You may also want to hold a famous farmer look-alike contest. Award a prize to the couple who looks most like a *Green Acres* couple, a *Hee-Haw* couple, or the couple on the old box cover for Kellogg's Corn Flakes.

Props: Hay bales make great backdrops for a barn blowout. If they are being placed on carpet, be sure to put plastic under them. You may also want to hang old farm implements on the back wall. Be sure to place all your props out in advance. The props for this game night are sure to arouse some curiosity.

Promotions: This game event works

great in conjunction with holidays associated with the harvest season. Many schools will have a harvest day dance, party, or celebration.

BOUNCE PONY RACES

Materials:

Ask around the church and find enough Bounce Ponies, Hopping Balls, or Harrison Horses to supply each rider with a horse. Cowboy hats add to the humor. Establish a course that passes through the audience. Instruct riders that no walking will be allowed, only bouncing and hopping.

The Challenge:

Cowboys and/or cowgirls mount their horses at a starting line. At a signal, riders must hop and bounce toward the finish line. Riders are not allowed to cross the line without their hats. This rule forces each rider to keep one hand on the hat and one hand on the pony, making it more difficult to keep themselves in motion. The first cowpoke to cross the line with a hat still on is the winner.

CHICKEN FEED

Materials:

Purchase a child's inflatable swimming pool for this contest. Fill the pool heaping full with popped popcorn. Hide five one dollar bills in the popcorn. Some costume and novelty stores carry chicken noses that can add further humor to this game.

The Challenge:

Use a signal like a triangle bell or cow-bell to start things off. At the signal, players put their hands on their hips and bend over to eat and to search through the popcorn. When a dollar bill is found, then play stops and points are awarded. Chickens must keep their hands on their hips at all times. Choose new chickens and go another round or allow the original chickens to peck until all five of the dollar bills are found.

COW MILKING

Materials:

Fill a surgical glove with milk and staple it to a sawhorse. This will be your "milking cow." Supply each team with a cow, a small bucket, a drinking glass, and a milking stool.

The Challenge:

Choose one farmer and one drinker from each team. Have the farmers sit on the milking stools beside the cows and puncture the finger tips on each of the surgical gloves using a straight pin or needle.

Ring a cowbell to start the action. Farmers will start squeezing the fingers of the glove to work out the milk into their buckets. When farmers think they have enough milk in their buckets to fill a glass, they run to the front of the stage where their teammates wait with the drinking glasses. The farmer pours his bucket of milk into the drinking glass. If there is enough milk to fill the drinking glass, then the teammate drinks down the milk and is declared the winner. If there is not enough milk to completely fill the glass, then the farmer returns to milk

some more. The first team to fill and drink a glass of milk is the winner.

KISS-A-PIG CONTEST

Materials:

You have two game options here and both are hilarious. The first option requires that you get your hands on a live pig. The second option is to purchase one large plastic piggy bank for each contestant. The banks are then filled with a favorite soda or flavored drink using a small funnel. A piece of duct tape is placed over the coin slot and a small hole is punctured in the plastic between the lips of the pig (use a clean nail).

The Challenge:

For the first option, you must select in advance several volunteers who will compete for the opportunity to kiss a pig. Pastoral staff, favorite deacons, youth sponsors, and popular youths are all good choices. You then sell votes for who will have to kiss the pig. Whoever gets the most votes must kiss the pig.

With the second option, you call up one volunteer from each team. At a signal, each player tips the piggy bank and drinks the liquid through the hole in the pig's lips. Drinking through this hole gives the appearance that contestants are kissing a pig. The first player to finish all the drink is the winner.

NOODLE IN A HAYSTACK

Materials:

Ask a farmer for a few bales of hay and the use of a galvanized metal water trough. Most farmers will donate the hay and the use of the trough. If no trough is available, you can use an old bathtub or washtub. Break the bales into the tub and make a haystack. Hide some large, uncooked egg noodles in the stack.

The Challenge:

Select a contestant from each team. At a signal, have the contestants gather around your haystack and search for the noodles. The first player to find a noodle in a haystack is the winner.

A variation of this game involves having your contestants be on the alert throughout the entire evening. They are instructed to try and find a noodle each time they hear the sound of a cowbell. Once the signal is given, they have 60 seconds to search. Sound the signal several times during the evening, whenever the action gets slow. Award points each time a noodle is found.

PIG'N'OUT

Materials:

Prepare some "pig slop" in advance by mixing any reasonably edible combination of leftover food. Purchase a plastic pig nose for each player from a costume or novelty shop. Have school lunch trays or large heavy-duty paper plates to serve the pig slop on.

The Challenge:

Select a contestant from each team and seat them at a table. Dish out a plate of slop for each contestant and hand out the pig noses. At a signal, contestants eat the pig slop without using their hands. When they finish the slop, they are to jump up and yell, "Soo-eee!" The first contestant to finish the pig slop and give the pig call is the winner.

TONIGHT'S MESSAGE: THE FARMER AND THE SOILS

Scripture: Mark 4:1-20.

Introduction:

Most people in America have heard the Good News at one time or another. The following parable teaches us that our long-term response to the Good News is what really counts.

Focus:

Tonight we want to ask the question, "What has happened to your crop?" The Bible identifies **four possible outcomes** for the seed that was sown when you first heard the Gospel.

1. It can be eaten up. When we remain hard in our hearts to the Gospel, then the Devil comes along like a bird and eats the seed. This keeps us from ever producing fruit for God. Our hardness must be broken so that the seed can penetrate the soil of our hearts and bring forth growth and fruit.

2. It can dry up. Have you ever met someone who was really turned on for God—but only for about a week? You were really impressed by that person and the radical change that had taken place in his or her life until they just dried up and quit. Where there is no fruit, there will be no root. Too many Christians settle for a shallow commitment. We must become firmly rooted in Christ through prayer and the Word to produce a crop in the long run.

3. It can be choked out. There are many things that will try and choke fruitfulness out of our lives. Verse 19 of Mark 4 lists these as the worries of this life, the deceitfulness of wealth, and the desire for other things. We must keep our focus on seeking first the kingdom of God and his righteousness, or the powers, attitudes, and desires of this world will choke out even the best intentions.

4. It can yield a true crop. The seed that falls on the pure heart will bring forth much fruit. Since God promised that he would create in us a new heart, everyone has the opportunity to live a life pleasing to him. The one who endures to the end will be saved and will produce a crop that is good, fruitful, and pleasing.

Conclusion:

What happened to your crop this year? Have you lived a productive life for the kingdom of God? Has there been any fruitful evidence since you first believed in Jesus? Each person should allow God to do a work in her or his heart that will guarantee a good crop. Each person should maintain a spirit of brokenness, a desire to be firmly rooted in Christ, and a proper eye toward that which is temporal and that which is eternal. What happened to your crop?